Gray Jolliffe

WICKED WILLIE

RELOADED

PRION

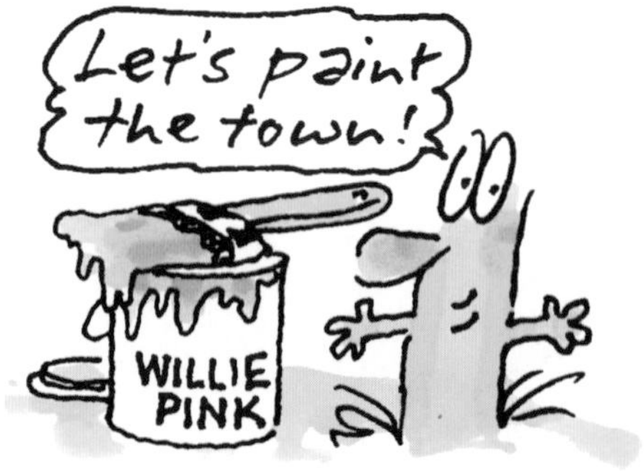
Let's paint the town!
WILLIE PINK

First published in Great Britain in 2004 by Prion Books
An imprint of the Carlton Publishing Group,
20 Mortimer Street,
London W1T 3JW

ISBN 1 85375 541 9

A CIP catalogue record for this book is available from the British Library

10 9 8 7 6 5 4 3 2 1

Executive Editor: Roland Hall
Art Director: Darren Jordan
Production: Lisa French

Printed in Singapore

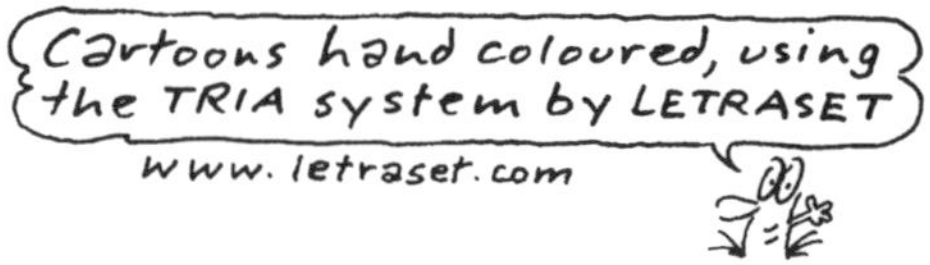
Cartoons hand coloured, using the TRIA system by LETRASET
www.letraset.com

Introduction

Willie, meet the person reading this book... Person reading this book, meet Willie...

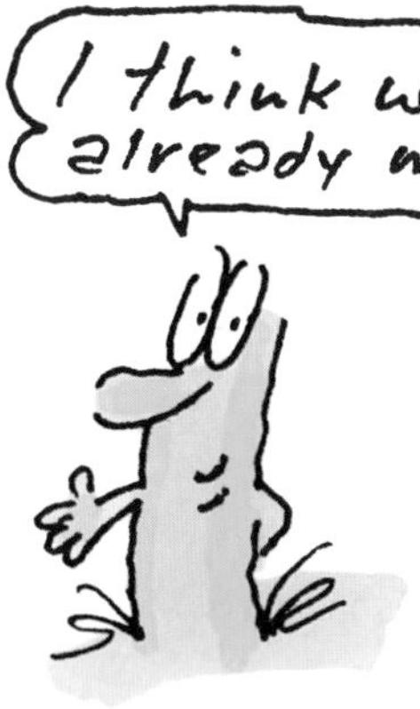
I think we've already met

Not a lot of people know this, but Wicked Willie not only has a mind of his own, but he has also insidiously infiltrated man's brain to the extent that he now has a permanent residence there, like some kind of special hotline to head office. As a result, males have become like one confused individual with two separate brains, which are either locked in terrible conflict or, at other times, best of pals.

Never mind what the psychologists say, with men it's not right brain and left brain – it's My brain and Willie brain.

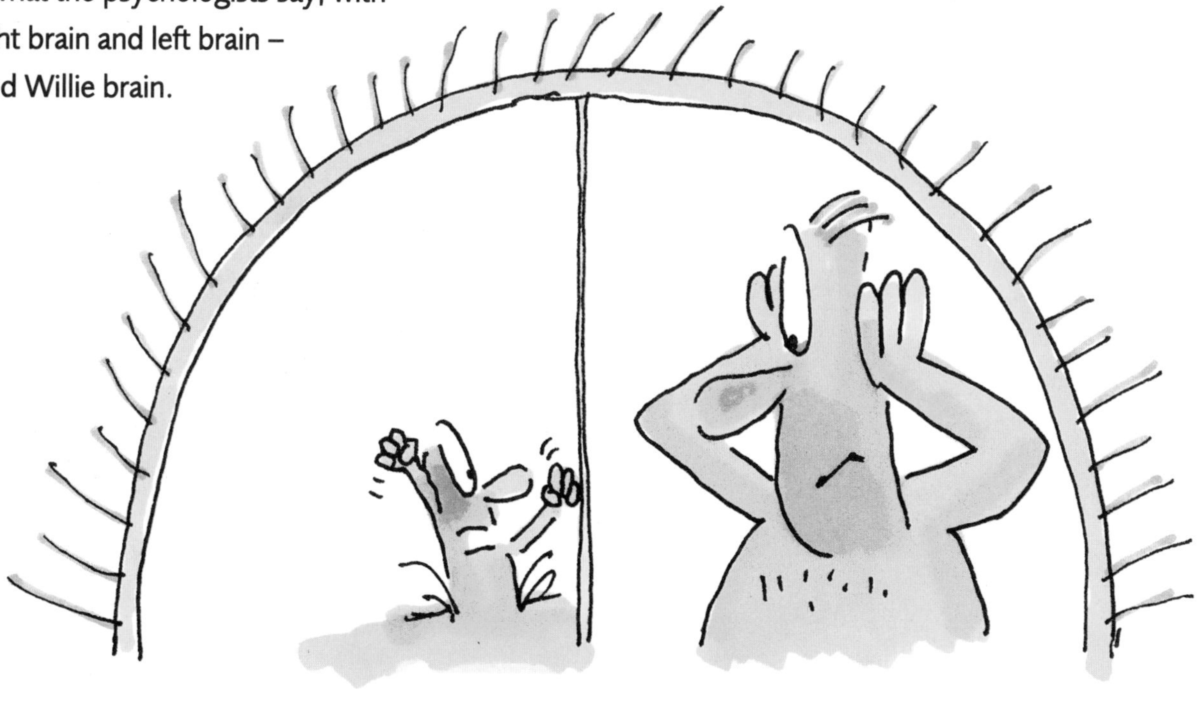

How it works

One of the secrets of success in life is having the right tool for the job, and that's exactly how Willie sees you. I don't want to worry you, fellas, but as far as he is concerned you are nothing more than an appendage, a means to an end – a slave who he orders to do his bidding. You not only get him to and from what he wants, but you bankroll his lifestyle as well. Only one man in history has dared challenge him – a very brave and talented painter who threatened to cut him off. But Willie got him by the goolies and forced poor Van Gogh to cut his ear off instead. That's the kind of tyrant he is.

Fifty per cent of the world's population is held under the spell of this character. That's a scary fact. But the real fact is we wouldn't have it any other way, because evil as he is, he's also a lot of fun!

We never agree 'cos I'm a Gemini and he's a nerd

PC GUIDE How to be TOTALLY inoffensive

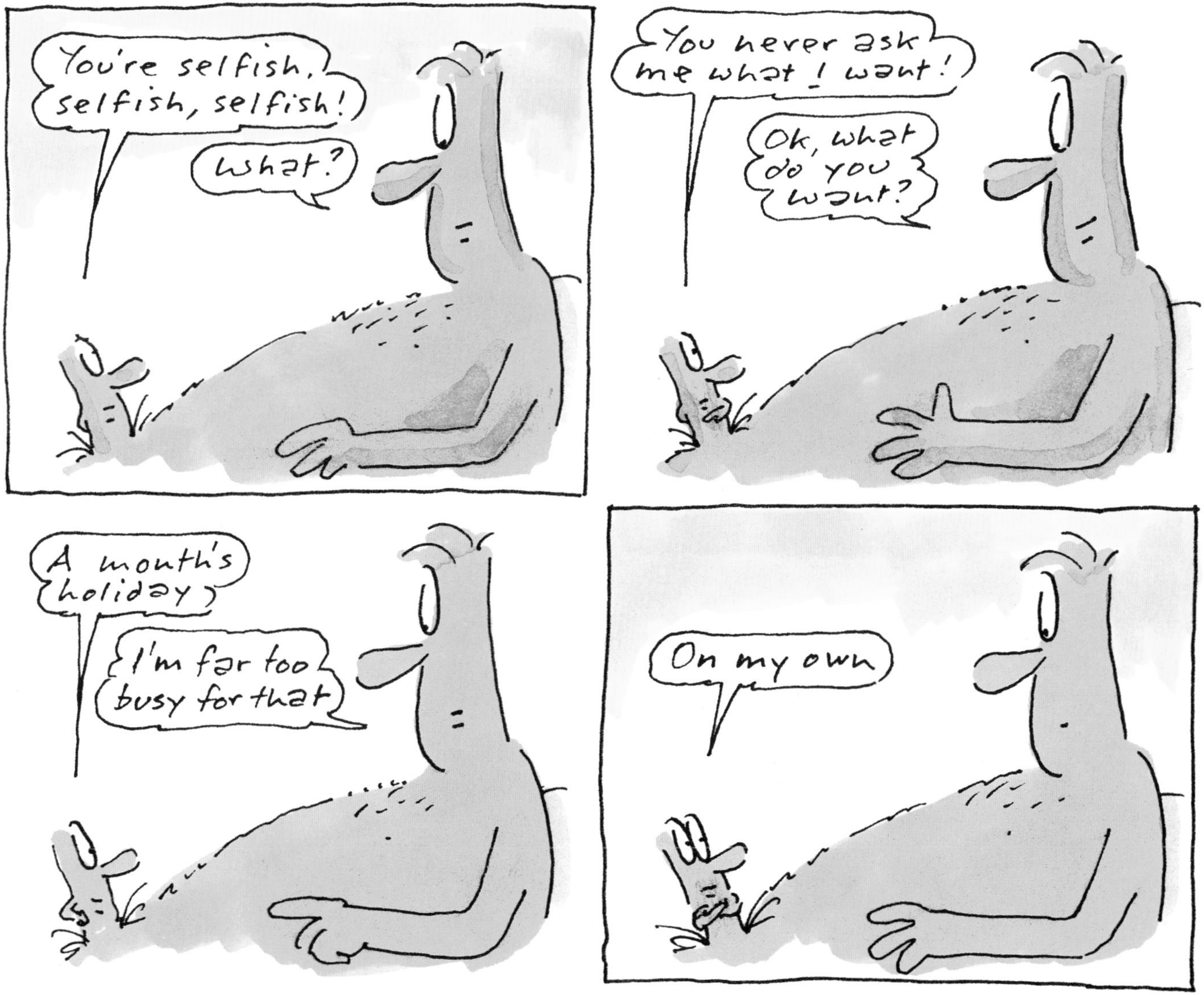
You're selfish, selfish, selfish!
What?
You never ask me what I want!
Ok, what do you want?
A month's holiday
I'm far too busy for that
On my own

Discovery

From babyhood men soon discover they have a wonderful toy attached to them. As we get a little older we also discover there is more than one use for it, and of course that is when the trouble starts. Realizing that the other half of the population is different in some fascinating way, a voyage of learning and seduction begins, led by the single-minded trouser tyrant. To get what he wants he relies on you to provide the sex appeal, the wit and the charm. He has no concept of seduction or the gentle approach. He thinks subtle is the opposite of stiff.

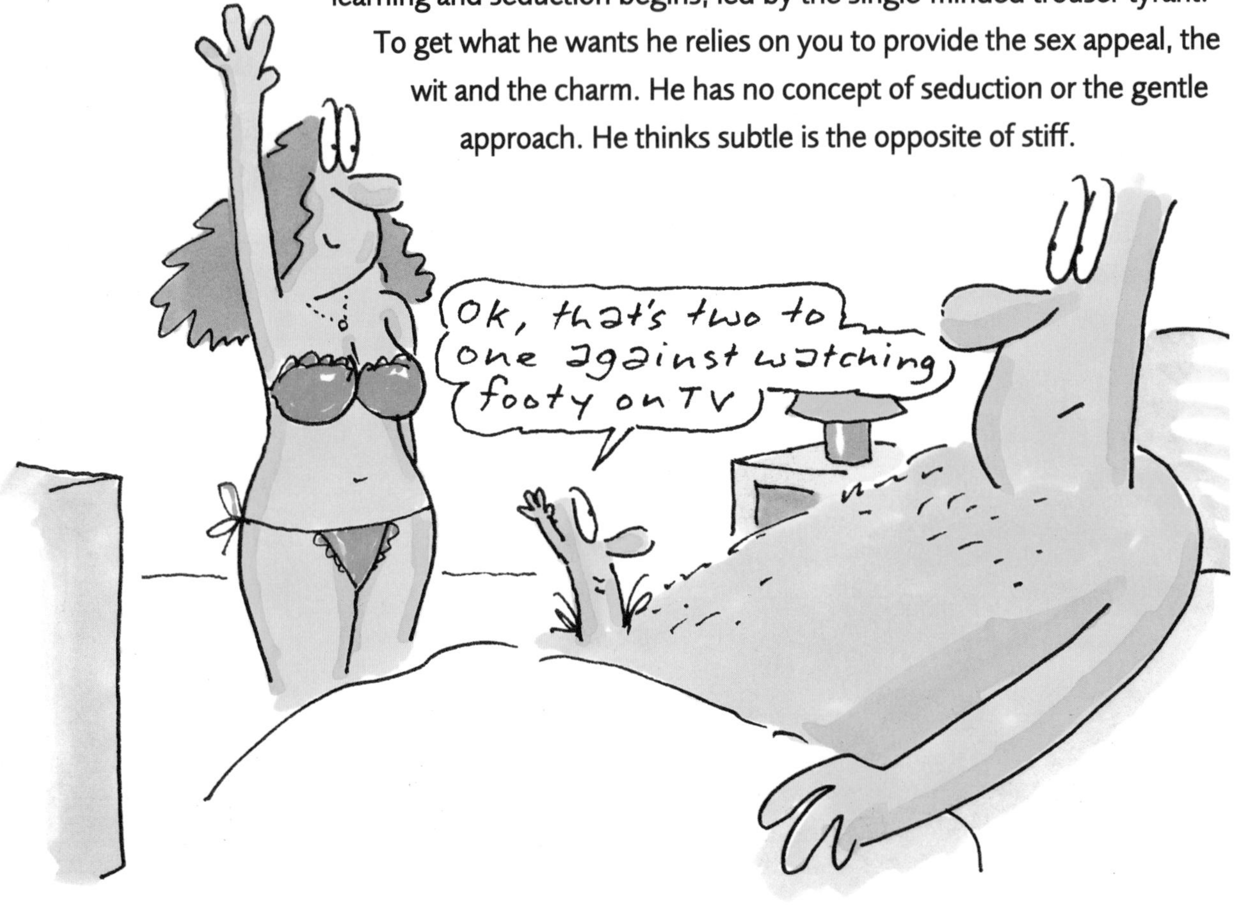
Ok, that's two to one against watching footy on TV

He never sleeps

You sleep, he tries to wake you. In the morning, even if you're not, he's ready to go to work – on your girlfriend, your wife, your hand even. Mainly your hand. At work you may have your eye on the CEO's job, but he has his eye on the CEO's personal assistant. In this continuous conflict of interests Willie usually wins because remember, he's up there in your head shouting at you through a very thin wall. So while success may elude you, you'll get some very happy memories in the process.

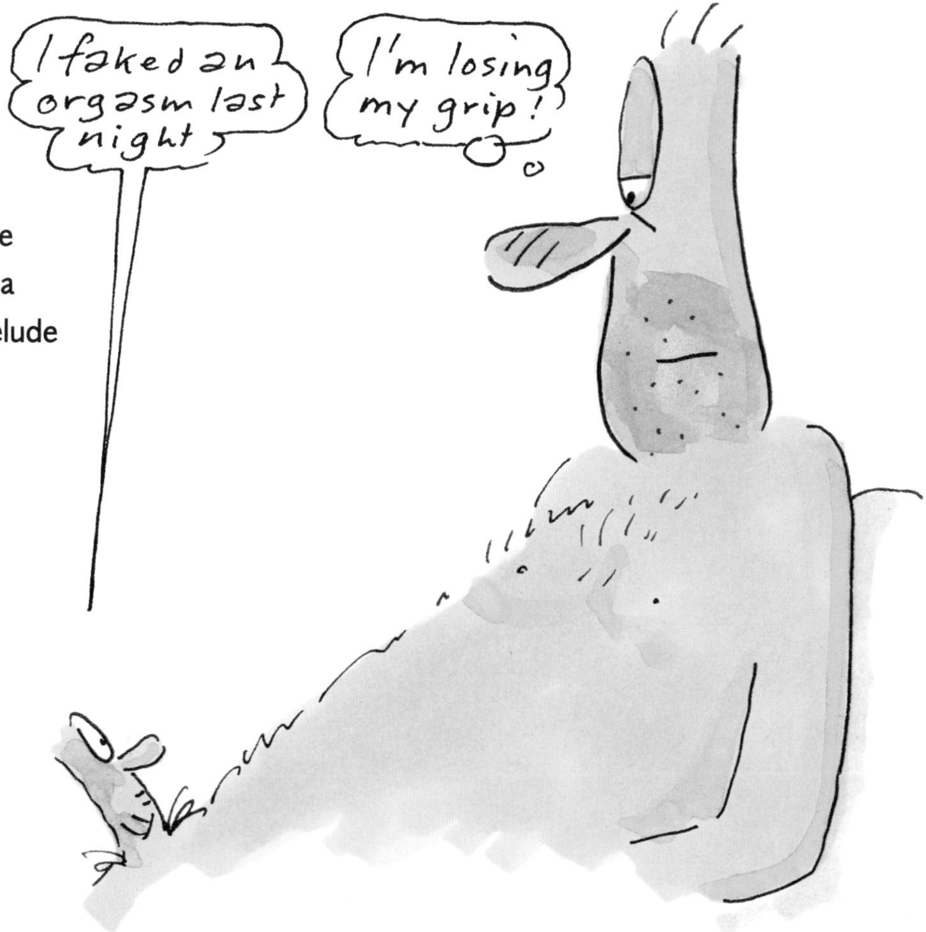
I faked an orgasm last night
I'm losing my grip!

Blame Willie – it's all his fault

No matter what you set your mind to do, the selfish little villain does everything he can to take your eye off the ball and direct your energies elsewhere. Whatever you do, calamity is waiting with open arms for Willie to drag you towards it.

It is a statistical fact worldwide, (so they say) that at the end of every social gathering involving both sexes – parties, dances, orgies, whatever – at the end there is always a girl in tears. And why? Because WW is constantly haranguing his slave to flirt with anyone in a dress or with bumps on the front and this leads to weeping and recriminations, fights and divorces. And more often than not, no sex. In this respect, though he may be Man's Best Friend, he is his own worst enemy. An idiot in fact.

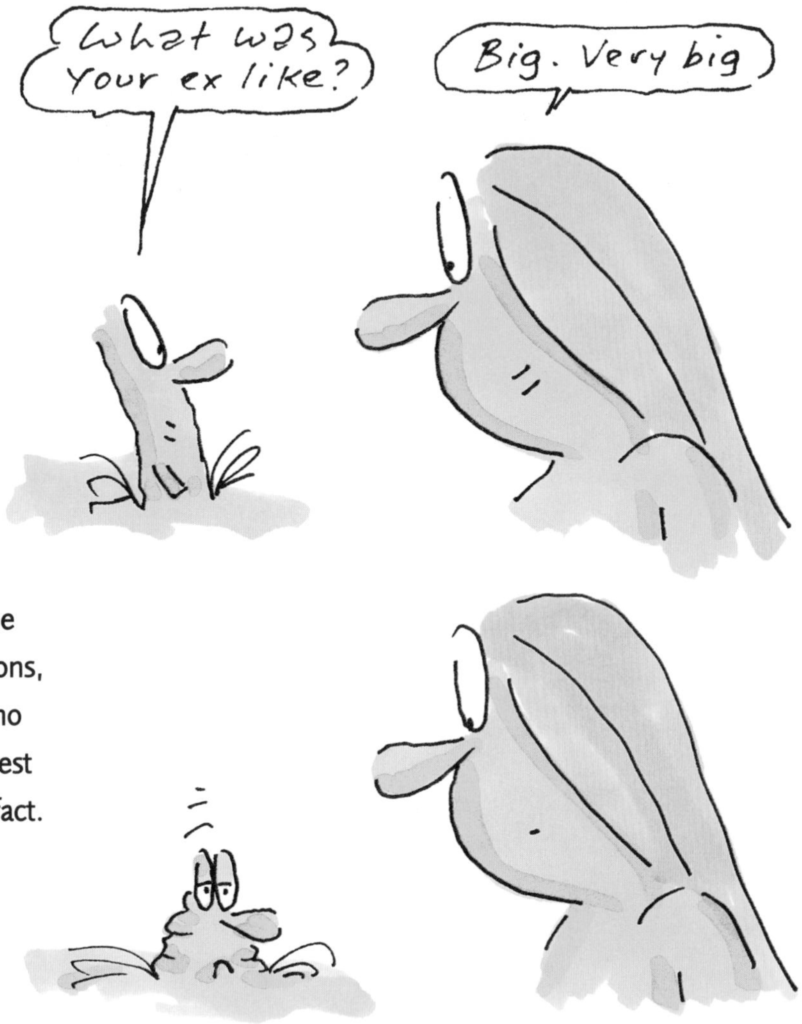
What was your ex like?
Big. Very big

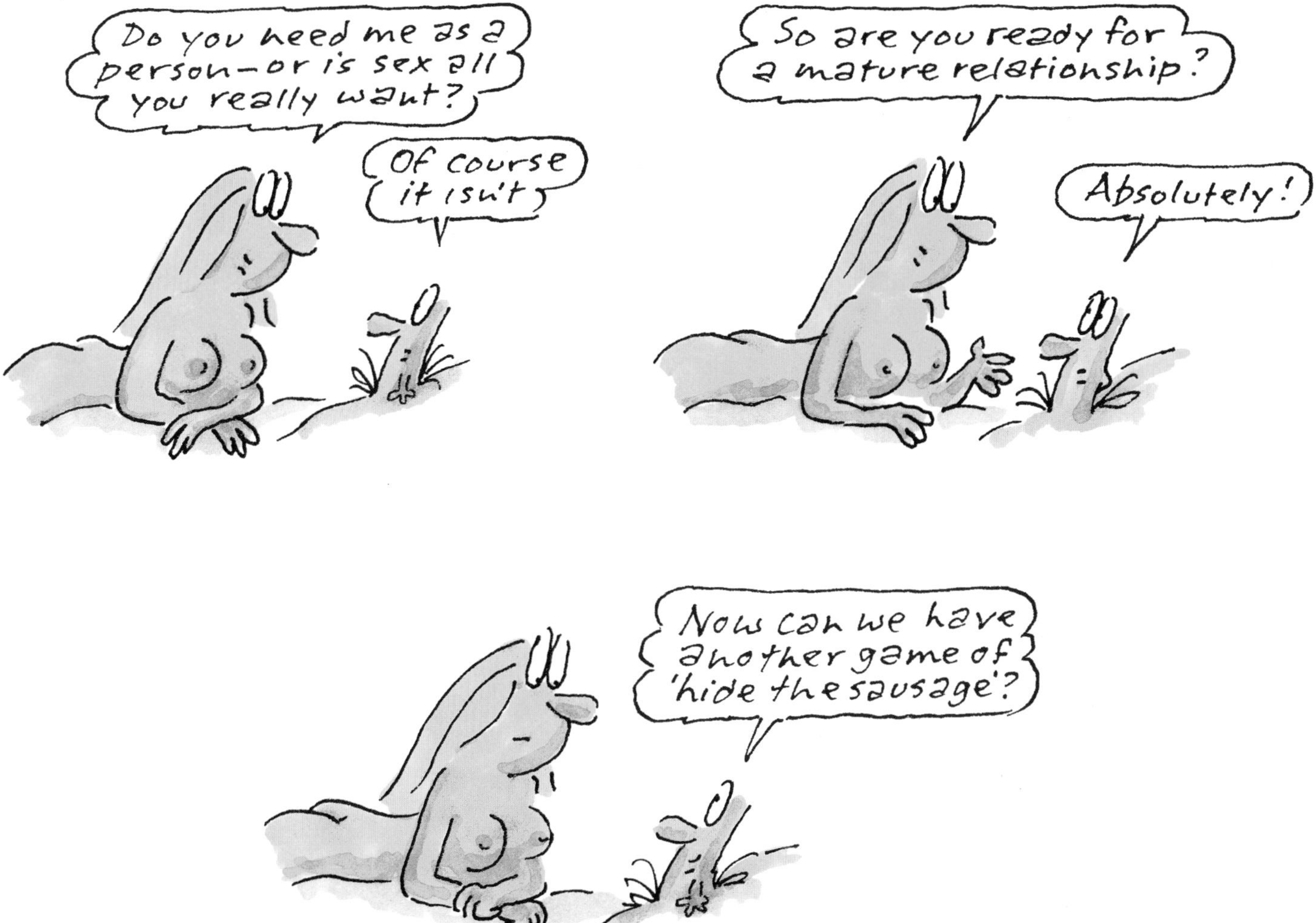
Do you need me as a person—or is sex all you really want?
Of course it isn't
So are you ready for a mature relationship?
Absolutely!
Now can we have another game of 'hide the sausage'?

The road to ruin waits for all men

Willie's ego is out of all proportion to his body weight and leads us all to boldly go on an endless sex trek. Respectable men are sucked in to dangerous liaisons of all kinds. You only have to read the tabloids – ruined politician, exposed footballer, de-frocked priest, struck-off doctor, guilty judge, even US Presidents – splashed all over frocks and front pages.

We all lie, we all deny, and the only one who comes clean is Willie. A trail of shattered careers and marriages, and all at the tiny hand of the pink pest in their pants. It's incredible, but true – once Willie tugs us towards the fulcrum of the see-saw, the balance slips and the inevitable downhill slide goes right into tomorrow's headlines.

He is pre-programmed by Mother Nature (of all people) to desire and have as many women as he can fit in a working day. The F-word in his vocabulary is eight letters long – 'Fidelity' – and he has absolutely no problem with loving eight women at the same time. So when a girl says, 'You're only interested in one thing,' the only honest thing he can do is deny it, although he knows what she means isn't what he means. But fortunately for civilization, Wicked Willie doesn't always get his own way.

Post this for me

Susie

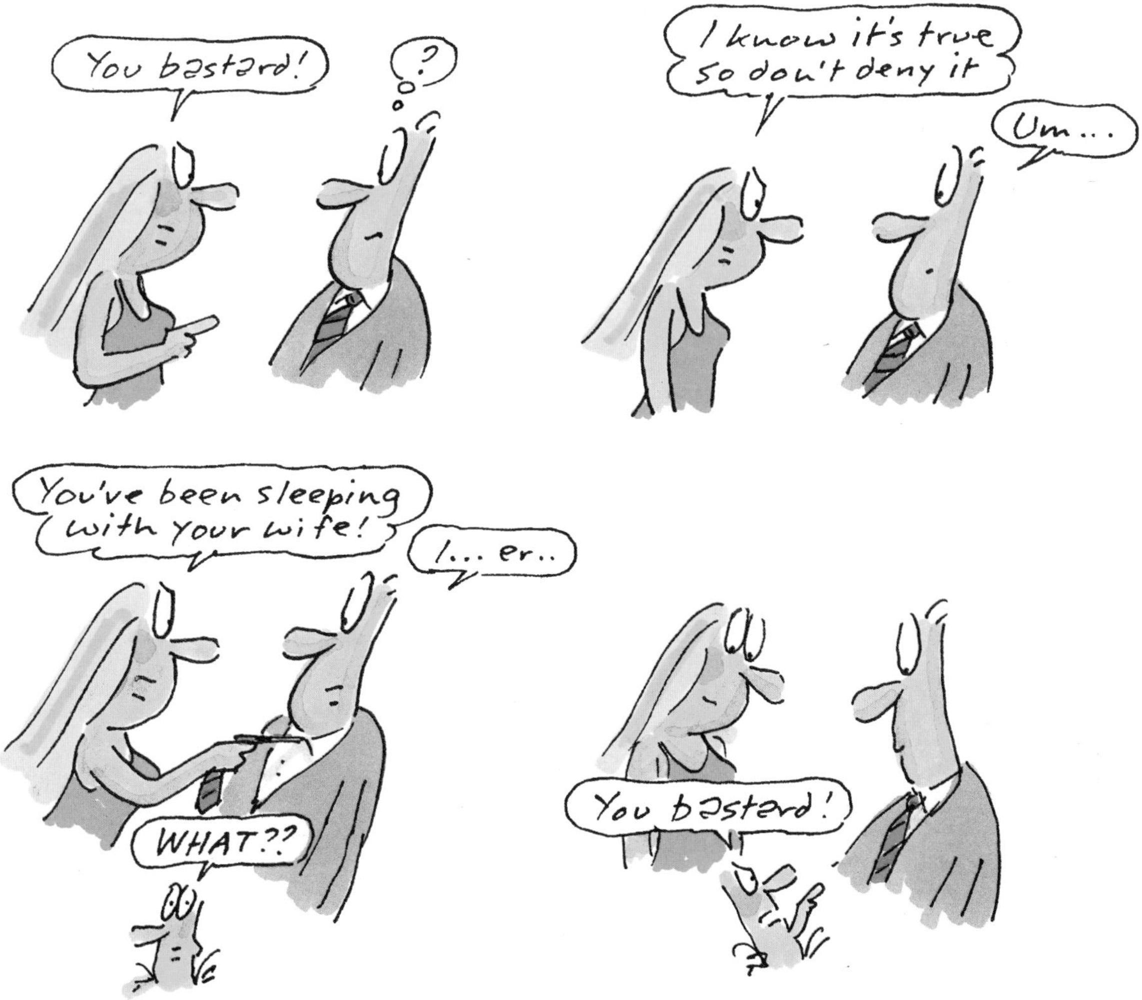
You bastard!
?
I know it's true so don't deny it
Um...
You've been sleeping with your wife!
I... er..
WHAT??
You bastard!

Love

It is said that 'Love is a tiger everyone wants to pet, but you can end up losing your head.'

Love goes very much against the grain with Willie, but occasionally – very occasionally – you get the upper hand and manage to persuade him that this time it's true love.

After lots of dates and romantic evenings with the divine object of your emotional as well as sexual desire, Willie's moment arrives, but instead of making the expected grand entrance he blows a fuse and forgets his part. Nothing happens. The strain of it all means he isn't in control for once and he limps offstage.

And now you have to explain to a surprised girl that he really does fancy her, and it will be ok next time. If there is a next time.

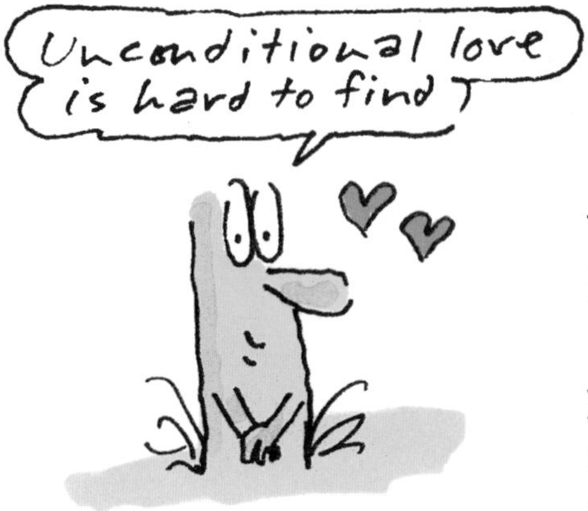
Unconditional love is hard to find

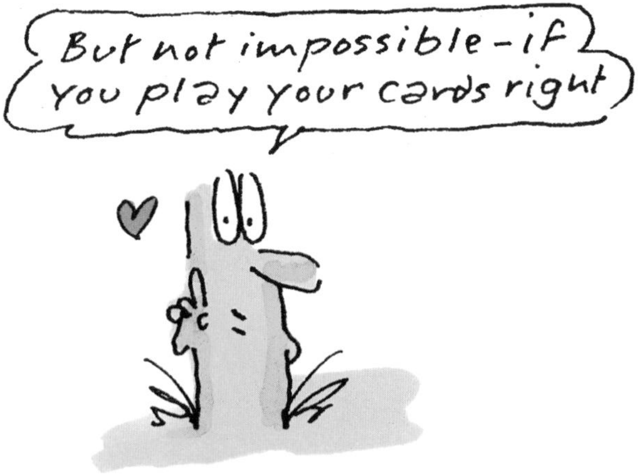
But not impossible - if you play your cards right

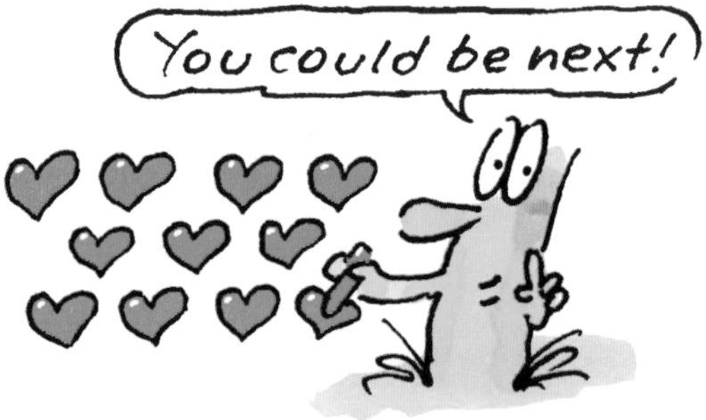
You could be next!

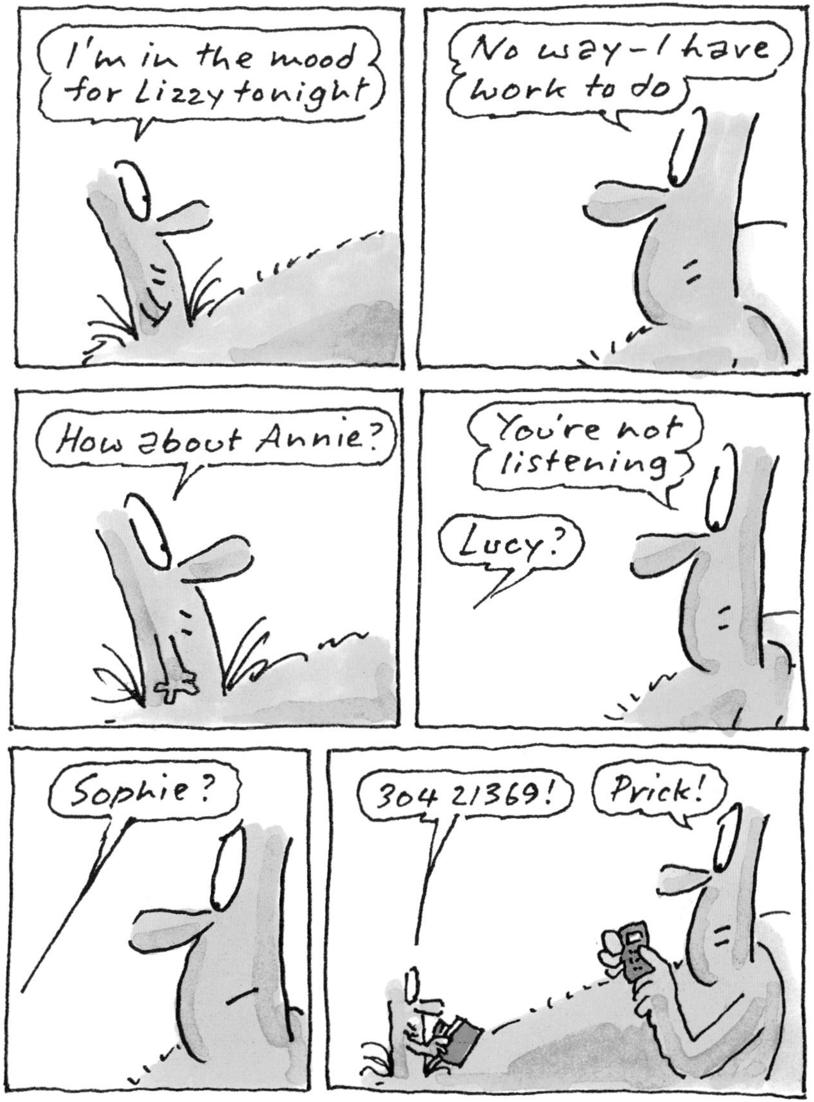
I'm in the mood for Lizzy tonight
No way - I have work to do
How about Annie?
You're not listening
Lucy?
Sophie?
304 21369!
Prick!

The odd couple

There is a basic understanding between man and his Willie, a tacit agreement that they will co-exist in a symbiotic relationship. Not that either has much choice, given the physical attachment, but even so they work better as a team, each using their own talents to form a mutually agreeable lifestyle.

They have become the odd couple: Sensible, sensitive man who hopes for the best but would never get laid if left on his own, and uncouth, testosterone-driven Willie who only wants to party and is forced to wait, drumming his little fingers while his unwitting slave is enjoying a movie, cocktails or a candlelit dinner.

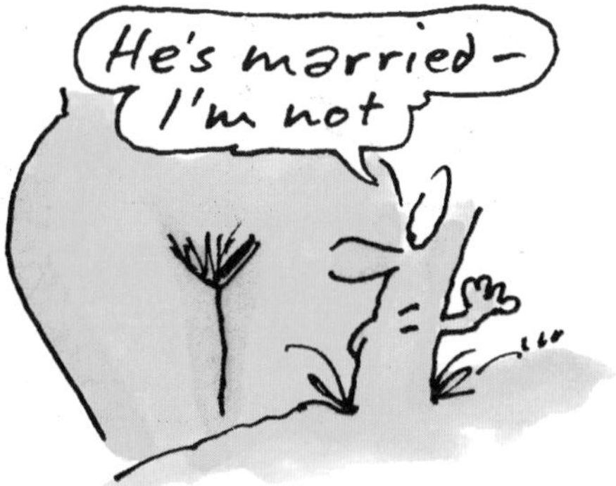
He's married -
I'm not

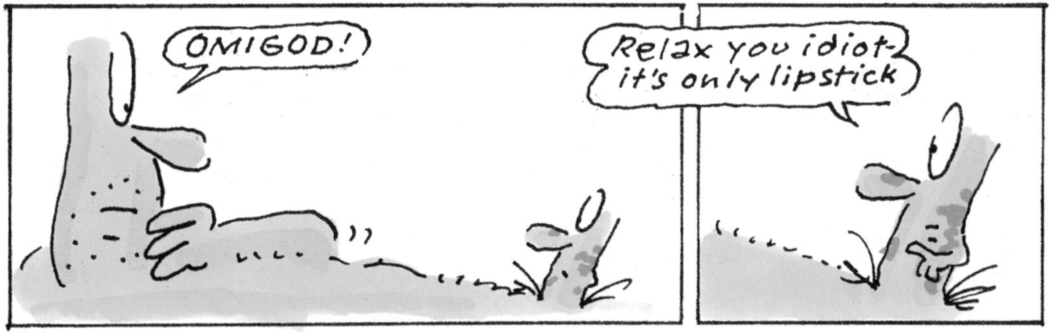
OMIGOD!
Relax you idiot-
it's only lipstick

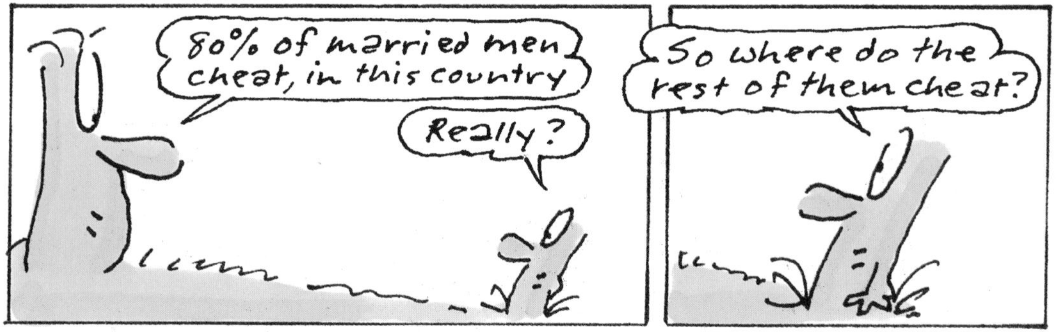
80% of married men cheat, in this country
Really?
So where do the rest of them cheat?

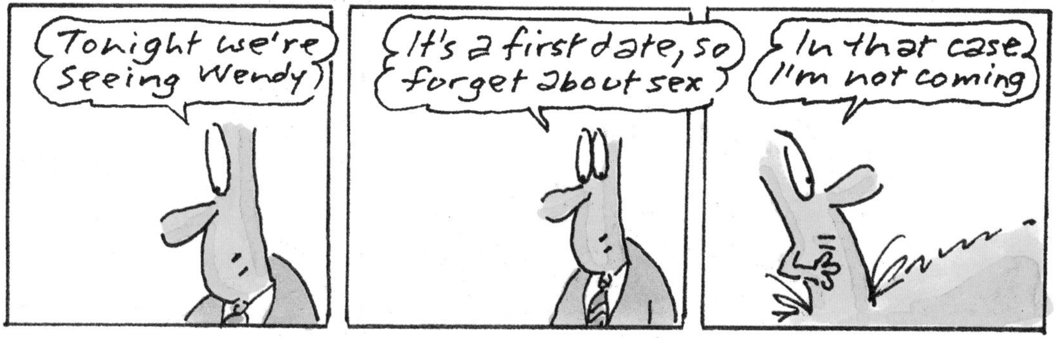
Tonight we're seeing Wendy
It's a first date, so forget about sex
In that case I'm not coming

Parties, public transport, pubs – the more crowded it is, the more Willie likes it. All the more chance to get up close and personal with the girls. He has only one thing on his tiny mind and he makes sure his man gets the message. He is by nature totally indiscriminate, but luckily his other half is there to veto, or at least fine tune, his more exotic sexual choices, and has the final say – or at least thinks he has. Either way they both like girls with lovely round bottoms.

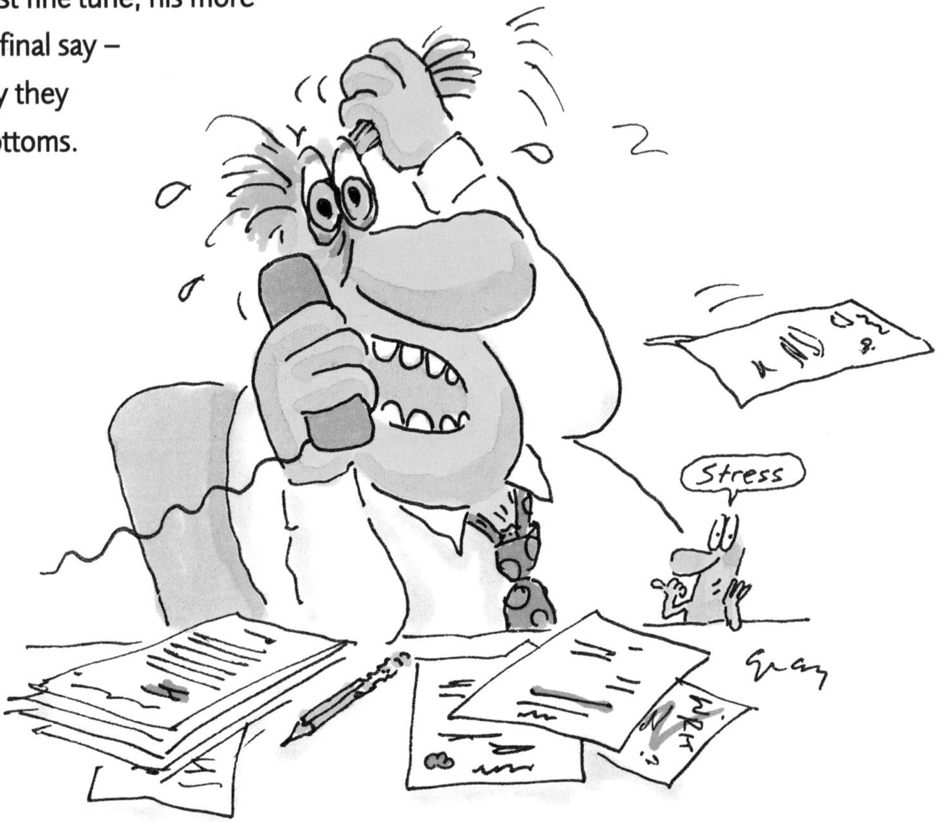
Stress

Willie can cost lots of money. The moment he gets fixated on someone he starts ordering champagne instead of wine and reserving tables at expensive restaurants. But guess who has to pay the bills?

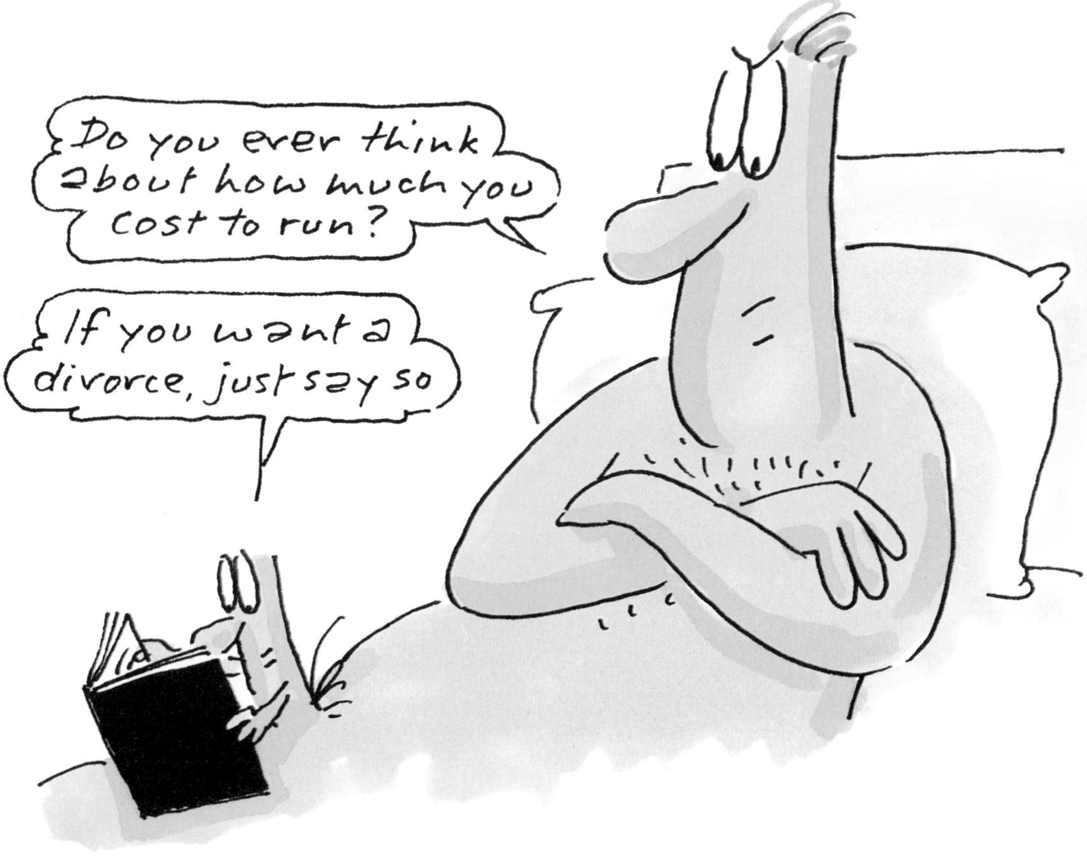
Do you ever think about how much you cost to run?
If you want a divorce, just say so

Looking back

Young Willie had a deprived childhood and the only thing that happened to him was getting laughed at by little girls on the beach. Other than that, he spent so much time in the confined surroundings of school shorts that he missed the conditioning his owner had to endure in his formative years.

Environment plays a huge part in forming sexual attitudes, so in later life Willie finds it difficult to understand why his owner/slave has to make a federal case out of what seem to be simple and straightforward opportunities to get lucky.

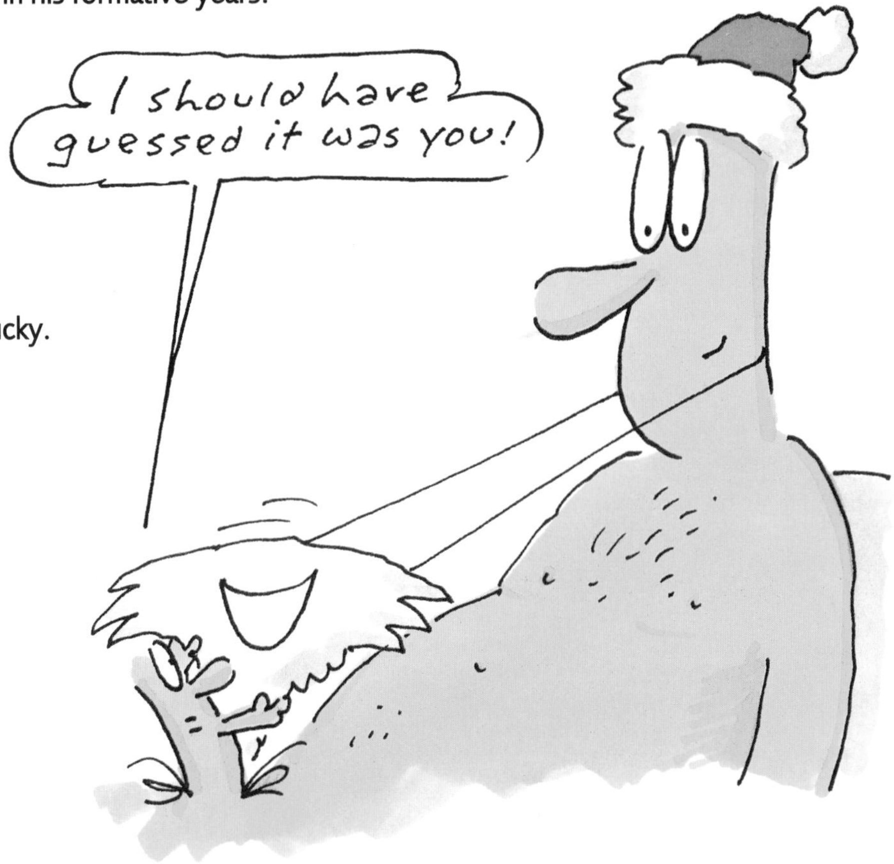
I should have guessed it was you!

When in the bloom of youth, all it takes is for a girl to wiggle her lovely bottom to give you an instant stiffy. Willie does the only thing he's there for – adopts instant action mode – and embarrasses you in front of the other students with the tented trouser syndrome.

Fortunately, as time goes by, after a few years and many silent arguments, he stops doing it. Except sometimes when you're slow dancing.

Everything Anthea does in bed is wrong
Stop moaning – the last one didn't do anything at all

I don't understand women
Do you understand electronics?
No
Doesn't stop you watching TV

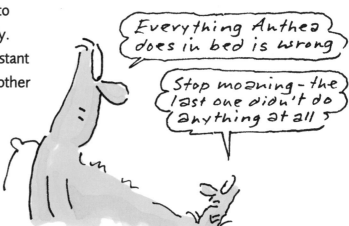

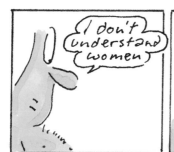

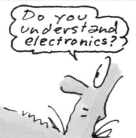

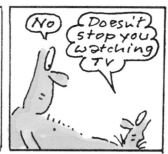

Basic differences between the sexes

There are many books on the subject. They are all boring. And earnest. Does it really matter? No. Willie's advice is to just get on with it.

When a woman feels sick or has a headache or is in a 'bad place emotionally' or just plain can't stand the sight of you, the last thing she feels like is sex. It's a shame the same can't be said of men, but you see, that would be reckoning without the one-eyed milkman.

No matter how sick a man is, hungover, run over, riddled with flu, food poisoning, car crash lacerations, broken bones, bereaved, fired, amputated or in the company of a woman he dislikes, he will still get a stiffy. Particularly in the company of a woman he dislikes. It's a kind of compensation, and Willie is there to take your mind off almost any ailment or misfortune, which is a good thing when you come to think about it, and explains why, when you're being loaded into an ambulance, you make a grab for the nurse. So one can't help feeling sorry for the girls who under similar circumstances have to make do with chocolate or shopping.

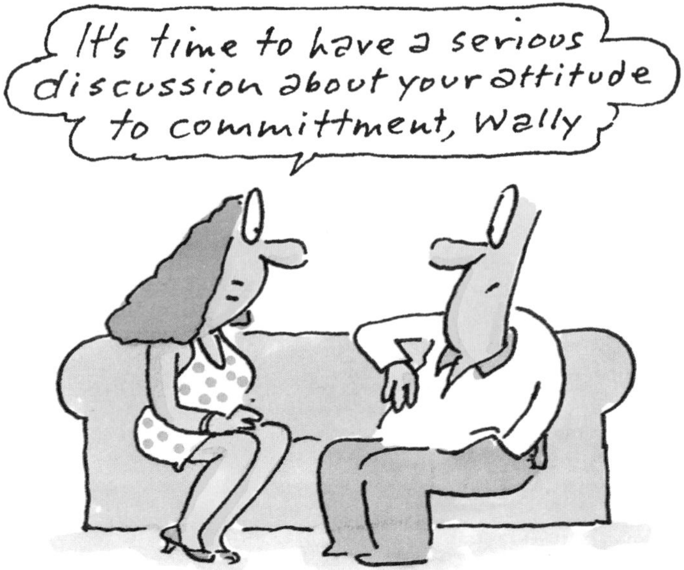
It's time to have a serious discussion about your attitude to committment, Wally

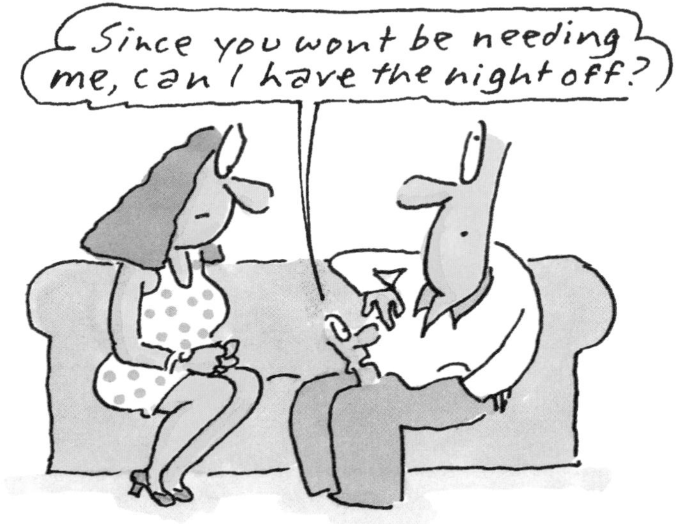
Since you wont be needing me, can I have the night off?

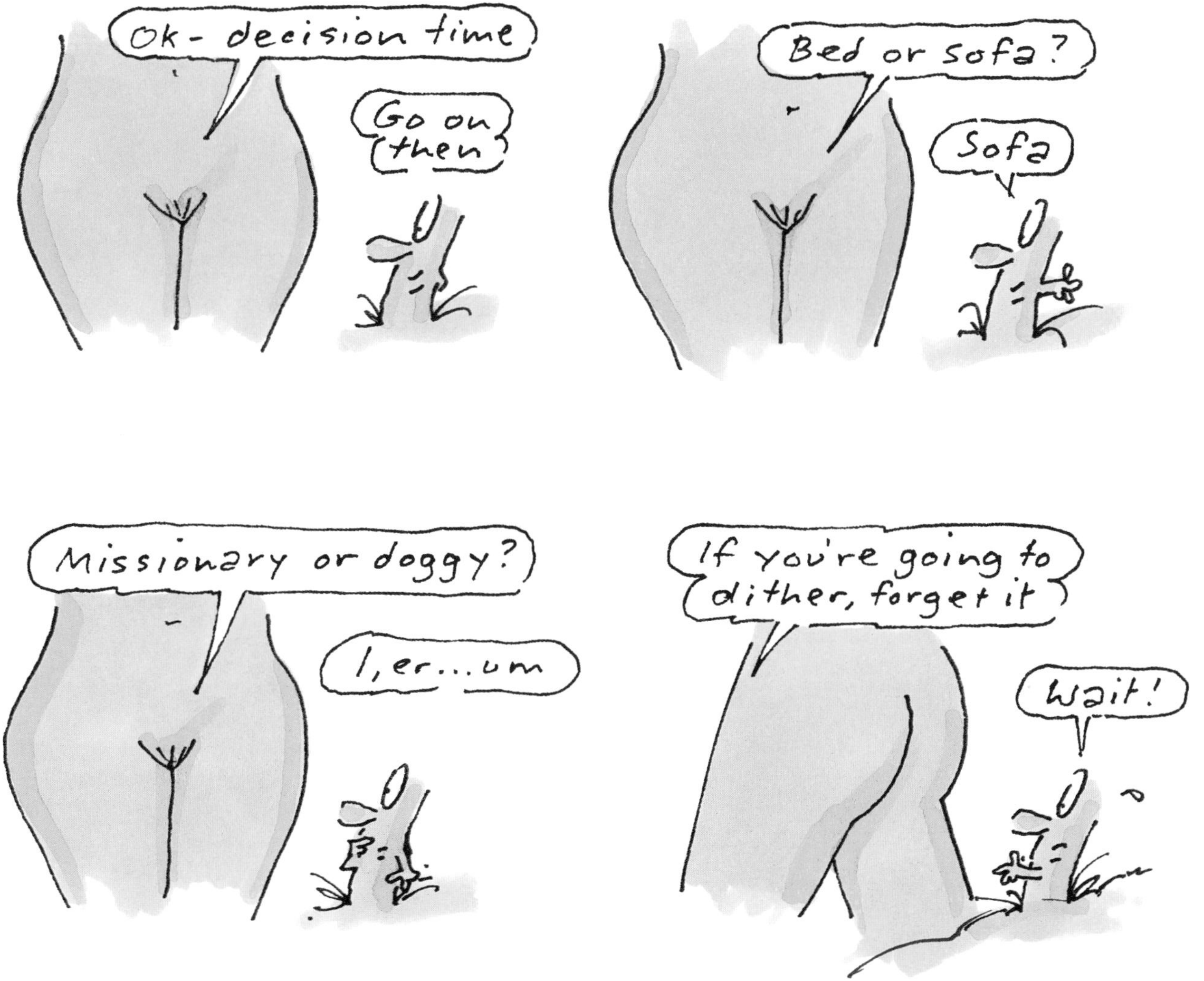
Ok- decision time
Go on then
Bed or sofa?
Sofa
Missionary or doggy?
I, er...um
If you're going to dither, forget it
Wait!

Shopping

If one had to sum up the difference between the sexes in only one word, this would have to be it.

To woman, shopping is the most effective aphrodisiac on the planet. To man it is the biggest turn-off. So stick that in your Mars and Venus.

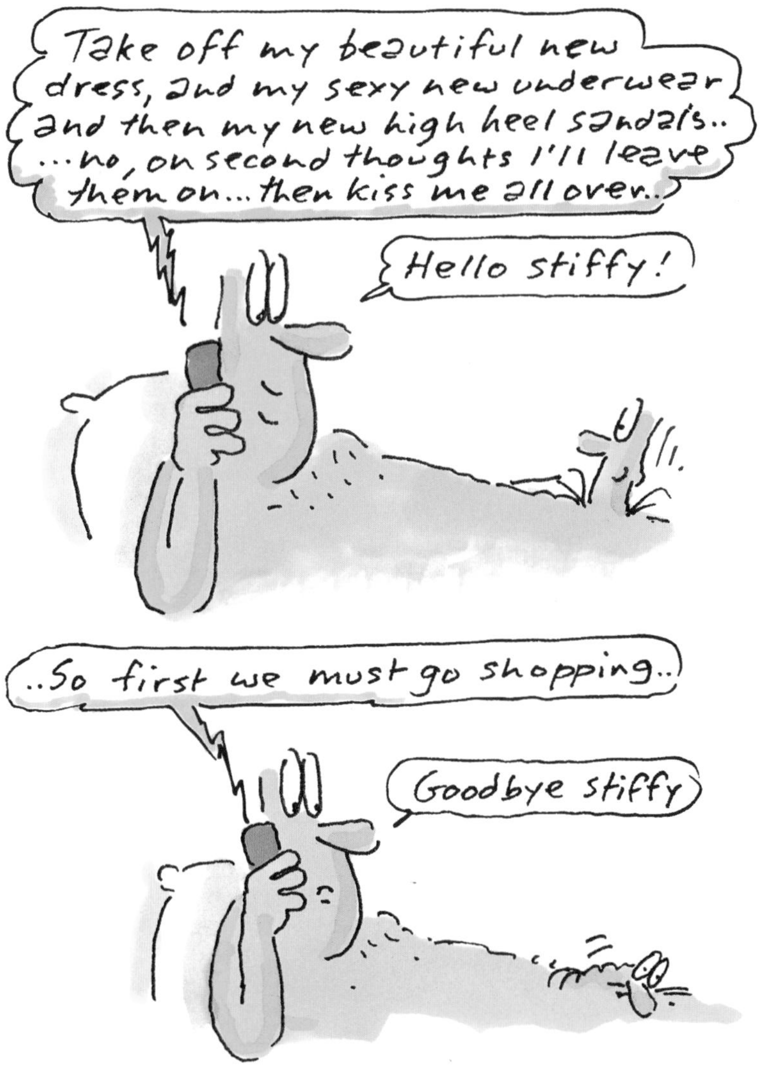
Take off my beautiful new dress, and my sexy new underwear and then my new high heel sandals.. ...no, on second thoughts I'll leave them on... then kiss me all over..
Hello stiffy!
..So first we must go shopping..
Goodbye stiffy

Willie on women

Willie understands only too well that women have cornered the market on, you know, pussy. They own 100 per cent of it and have a fair idea how desperate men are to get their hands on some. Considering the fundamental gap between us and the permanent undercurrent of distrust, it's a very fortunate thing for men that women don't own other life-giving commodities, like the air they breathe and the beer they drink, or their very survival would be at risk.

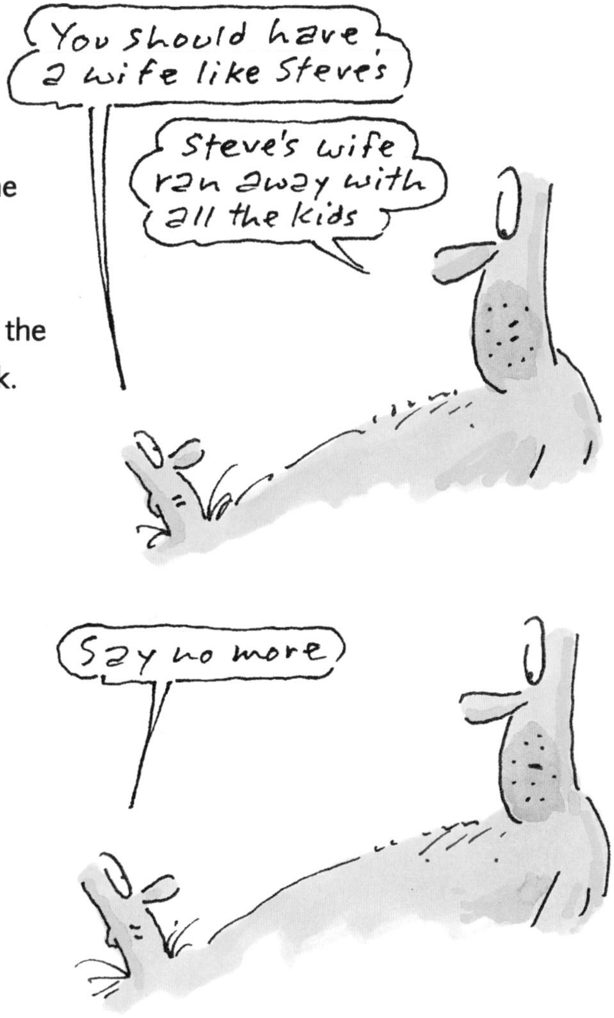
You should have a wife like Steve's
Steve's wife ran away with all the kids
Say no more

But luckily women are nicer than that, they don't let the power they wield go to their heads, and are generally helpful throughout negotiations, settling for little more than love, commitment, marriage and a takeaway. A few bad girls on the other hand, instead of sharing their wonderful gift, use it as a currency to bargain with. Not all that surprising really.

Mind you, if women really knew what was going on in the reprehensible minds of the odd couple, they would certainly be tougher to deal with. What men want is fairly basic. What they want is a warm girl in a tight top, a short skirt and high heels. And, naturally, a loving disposition. Willie's list of desirable qualities goes something like this:

* Anything that gives him a stiffy.
* Pissed and willing.
* Anything he hasn't already had.
* Fat girls with dirty eyes who are gagging for it.

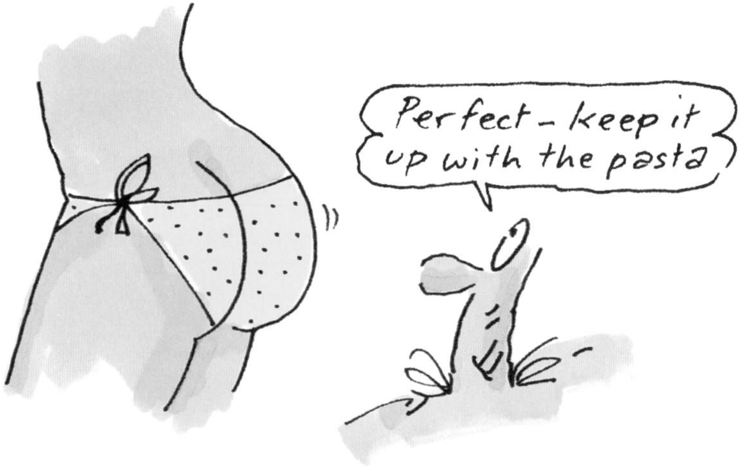
Perfect - keep it up with the pasta

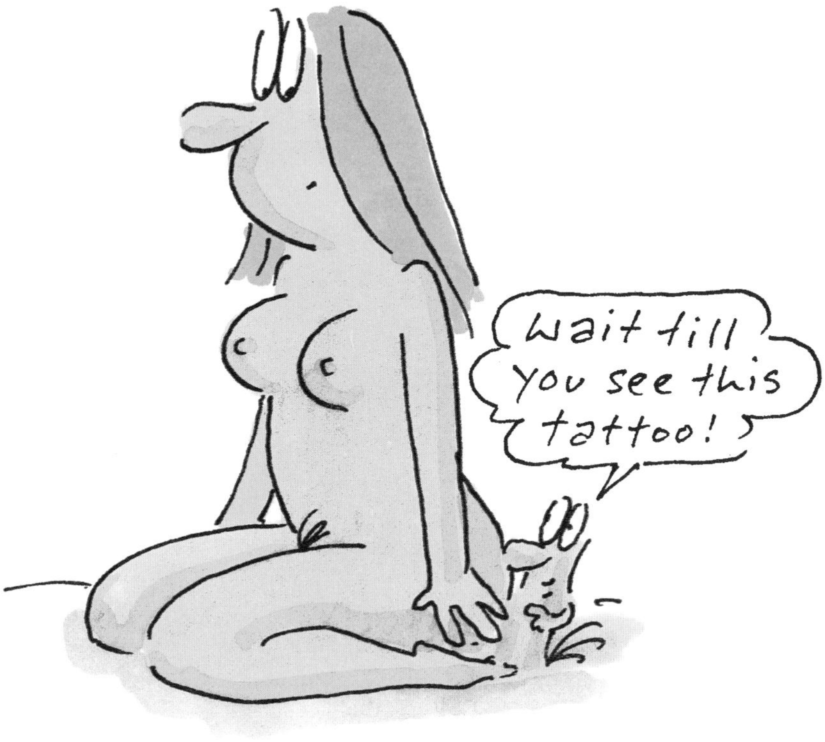
wait till you see this tattoo!

Willie's more civilized half, however, has a far more responsible attitude and his list of great female qualities goes more like this:

* Cheerfulness.
* Likes me.
* Likes sex.
* Is not cross when you fall asleep afterwards.
* Likes it often.
* Even in the morning.
* Does oral stuff while I'm driving.
* Looks astounding.
* Shops on her own.
* Um... that's it.

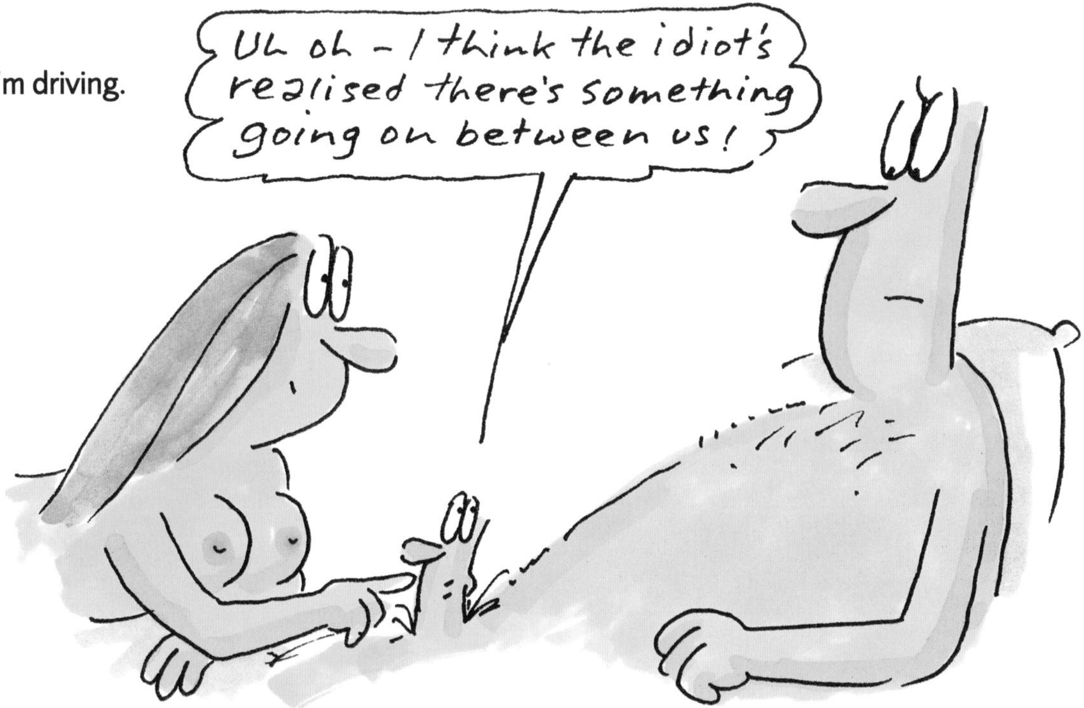
Uh oh – I think the idiot's realised there's something going on between us!

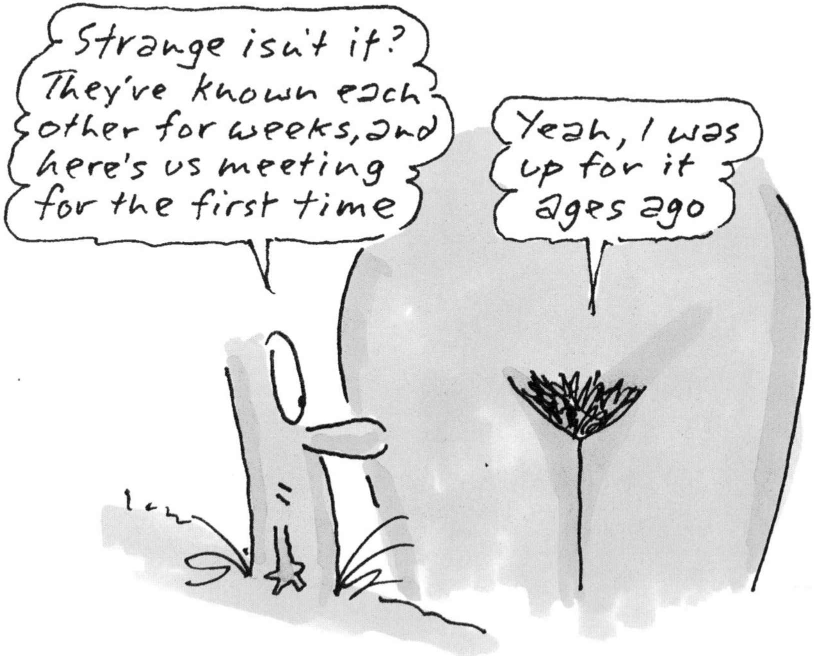
Strange isn't it? They've known each other for weeks, and here's us meeting for the first time
Yeah, I was up for it ages ago

Women – what to watch out for

This is Willie speaking, not the rest of us, so don't take too much notice. But anyway...

Women are intuitive. They can read a man's mind. They know when he's lying. Easy – he lies all the time.

Women soon find out what a man needs most and that's what they give him least of.

Penis envy. Forget Freud, there's no such thing. Women can get as many penises as they want, no problem. Trouble is, they don't seem to want that many. Women don't actually care about the size of a Willie unless they're so well off they don't have anything else to care about. As a rule, women have more serious priorities, like the width of his wallet. That's mean. Mean but true. But they tell their friends the size of his willie. And they tell him they don't go out with him for his money, then blackmail him into spending it all.

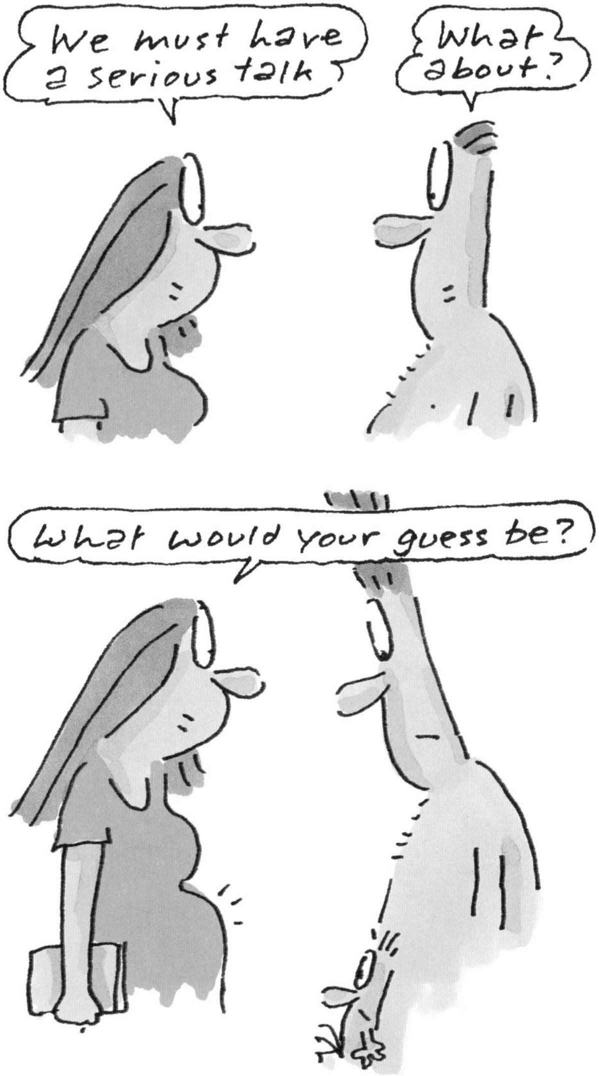
We must have a serious talk
What about?
What would your guess be?

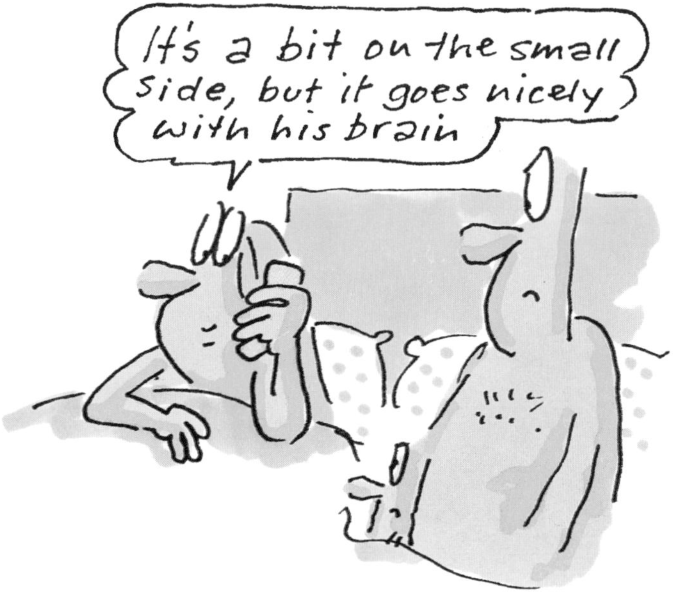
It's a bit on the small side, but it goes nicely with his brain

At home she complains non-stop that her tits/bum/legs are too big/small/fat/thin/short and says 'Yeccch, how could you fancy me?' When he assures her that he does, she says, 'Well you'd fancy anything.' True, but not what a man wants to be reminded of.

For Willie, a small percentage of women are to be avoided at all costs, however pretty they may be. He calls them 'lemon faces'. Lemon-faced women are never happy, whatever a man does. And no matter how many Chinese takeaways he treats her to, she never laughs at his jokes – even if they're funny. Other signs to look for:

Does her face look like a lemon? Chances are she's a lemon face. Does she look like a Pekinese trying to lick piss off a stinging nettle? Lemon face.

Has she got a body to die for? Then if she's a lemon face it's a terrible shame. A lemon face is an ideal date for a dedicated masochist.

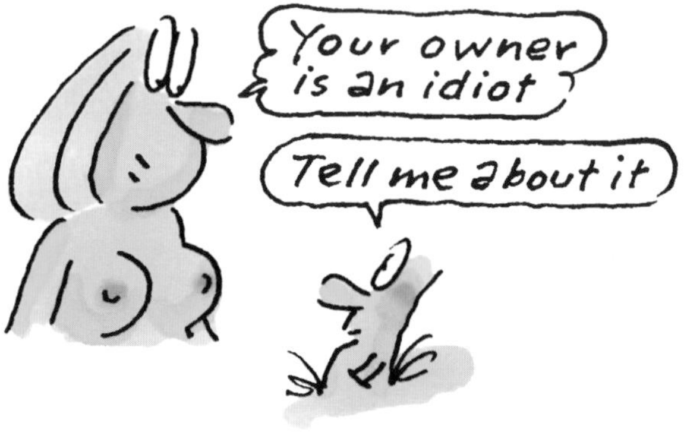
Your owner is an idiot
Tell me about it

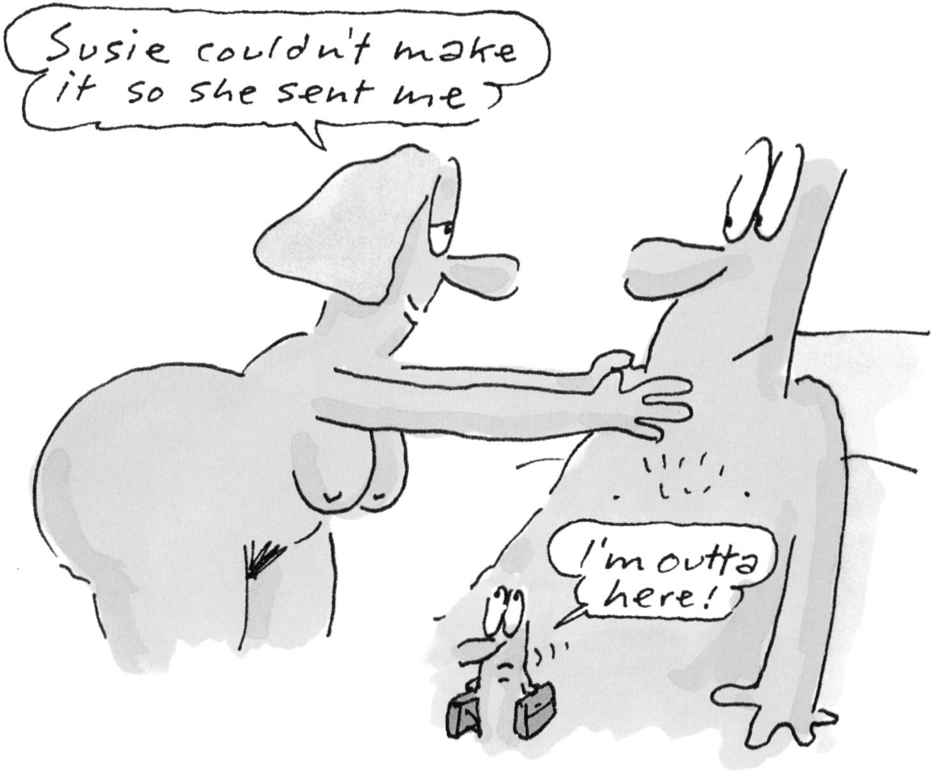
Susie couldn't make it so she sent me
I'm outta here!

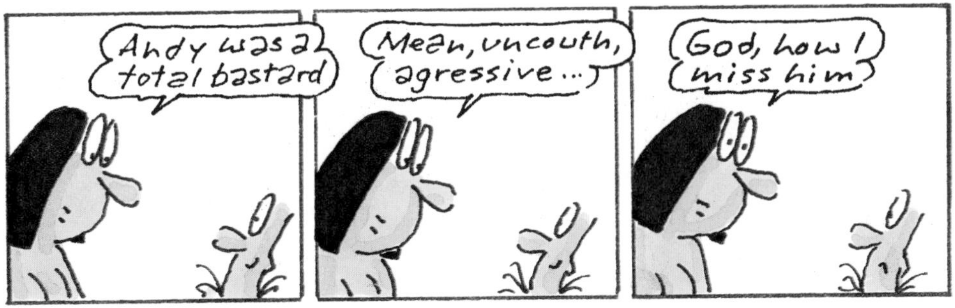
Andy was a total bastard
Mean, uncouth, agressive...
God, how I miss him

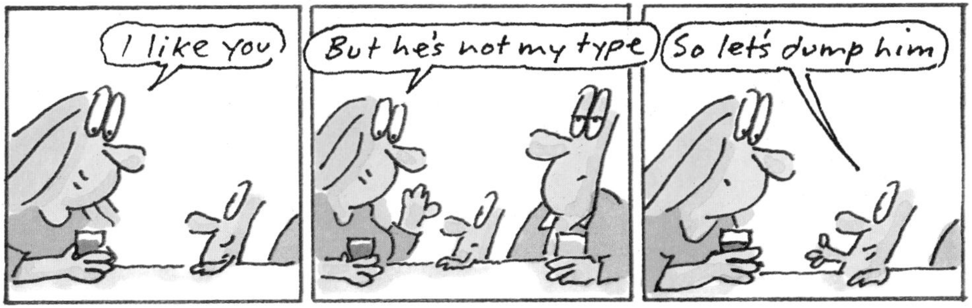
I like you
But he's not my type
So let's dump him

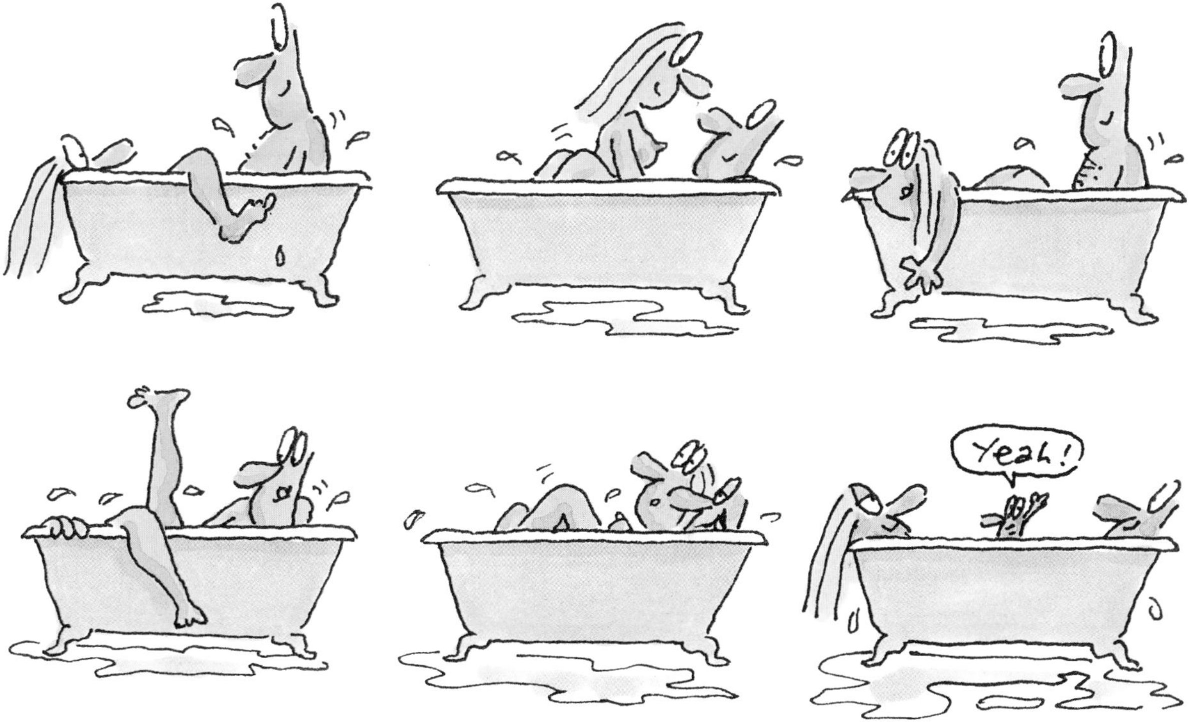
Yeah!

Sex tips for men

Willie is hardly an idealist when it comes to sex, but he knows that to get lucky, his slave has to know how to behave. Certain unacceptable habits must be avoided. Every man has his own brand of bad behaviour and the list is virtually endless. The following is but a small sample of things that can make a girl cut and run:

* Secret sniggering with your friends.
* Calculated vagueness.
* Drugged or drunk.
* Commitment phobia.
* Rational discussion.
* Foul language (other than when making love).
* Comments like 'reality is a hypothesis' and 'marriage? I'm an atheist.'
* Giving her a pet toad for Christmas.

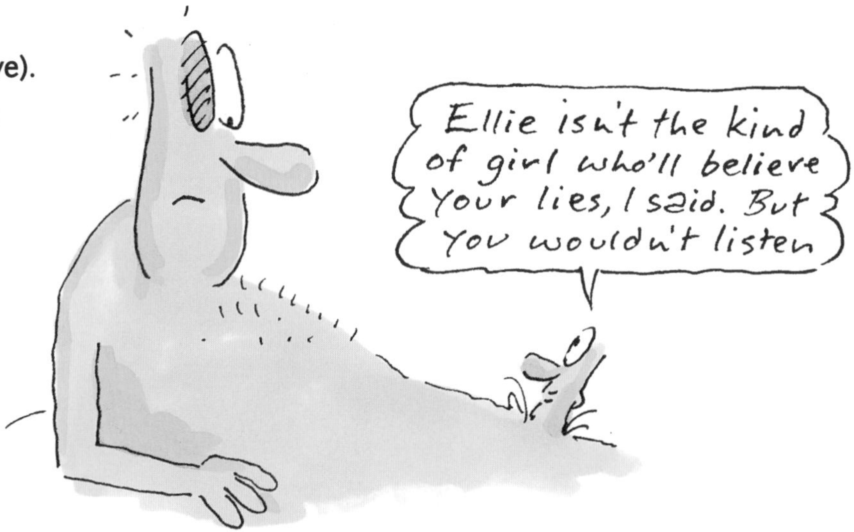
Ellie isn't the kind of girl who'll believe your lies, I said. But you wouldn't listen

These are a few of the most obvious turn-offs. Some women have been known to dislike a digit in the botty while in the throes of orgasm, but weird tastes are a whole new book.

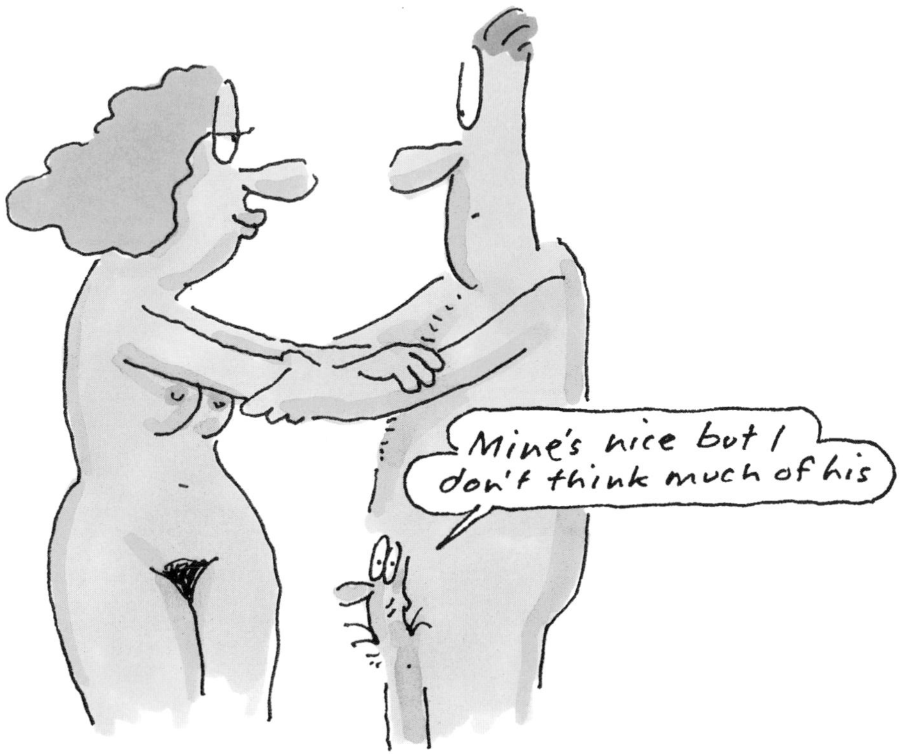
Mine's nice but I don't think much of his

Dating

Before a man asks a girl on a date he should take a look in a mirror and ask himself some frank questions. Am I fat and pimply? Ugly, bald and badly-dressed? Smelly feet? Halitosis that could kill a gorilla? Do I have warts on my willie? Is Willie a wart? Am I a criminal?

If the answer to any or all of the above is 'yes' you will be pleased to know that you will not only be attractive to women, but to beautiful women in particular. You only have to look at the wretches women go out with to realize the surprising truth in this.

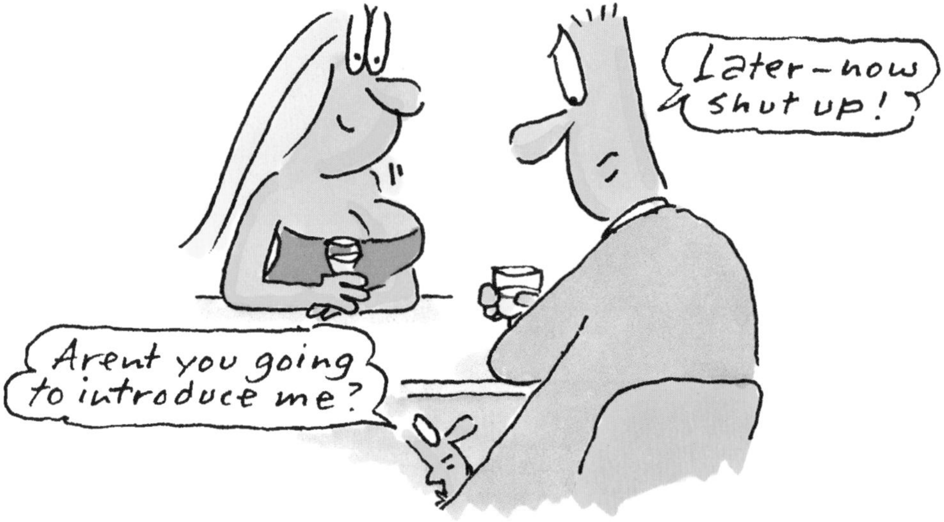
Arent you going to introduce me?
Later - now shut up!

Asking a girl on a date isn't easy, but you have to grasp the nettle. Just pick up the phone and do it. No, don't text her, talk to her. When she answers, don't say, 'Hi this is Nigel. I couldn't help noticing your tits and can I buy them dinner tonight?' Or you may well get a frosty silence followed by a click. She may not have realized it was only a Freudian slip – or you could have been talking to her mother by mistake.

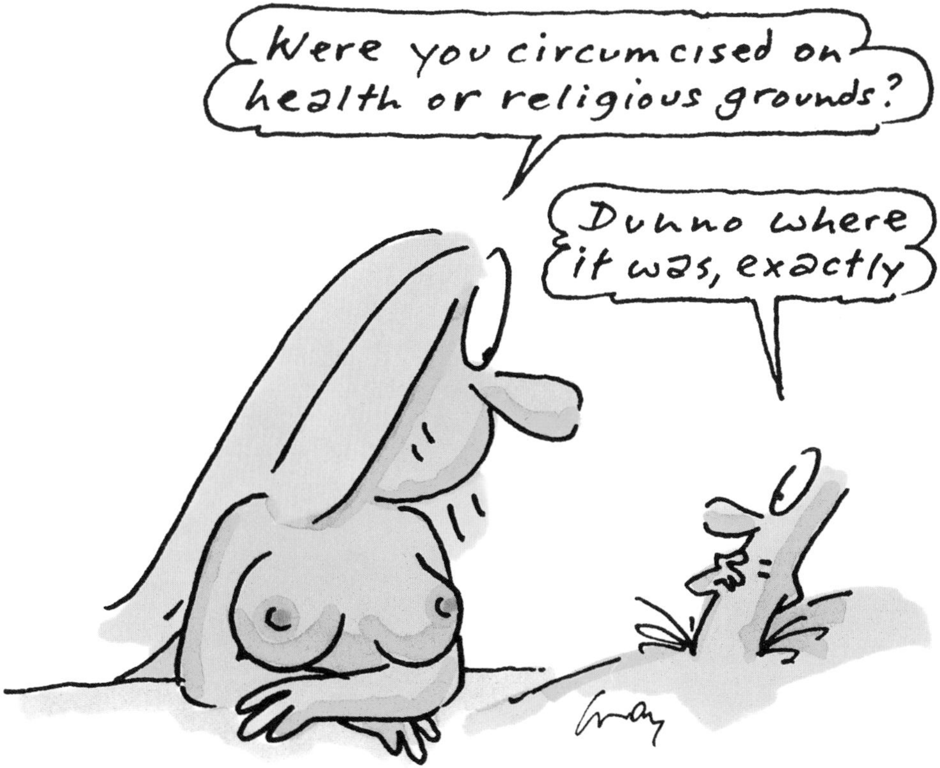
Were you circumcised on health or religious grounds?
Dunno where it was, exactly

First dates are more stressful than most things known to man. Ask yourself – do you have to look your best to be in a plane crash? Do you have to be witty when the stock market wipes you out? No, but on that first date?

The trick is to be yourself. Unless you are a total dork, in which case it's better to be someone else. And, unless you are desperate for rejection, the following phrases are best left out of your chat-up patter:

* You're not fat.
* My wife and I are having a trial separation while she's pregnant.
* Ever considered a breast implant?
* My last girlfriend was on the cover of *Cosmo* in a swimsuit, but don't worry – I'm not into looks any more.
* I don't suppose anyone has told you you're beautiful before.
* Sorry for fidgeting, but my piles are killing me – you know what it's like.

I can't believe someone of your beauty isn't a top model

Really? Shall we continue this discussion in your room?

Corny, but it worked

And some lines that shouldn't be heard from a woman are as follows:

* Mummy is dying to meet you. You're exactly her type.
* I've forgotten your name. Sorry.
* Yes, I'm six months pregnant – I'm really surprised you didn't notice.
* Yes, I'm six months pregnant – I thought that's why you asked me out.
* My last boyfriend had a teensy weensy one. It was less than seven inches!
* It's so nice to go out with someone who doesn't mind I used to be a man.

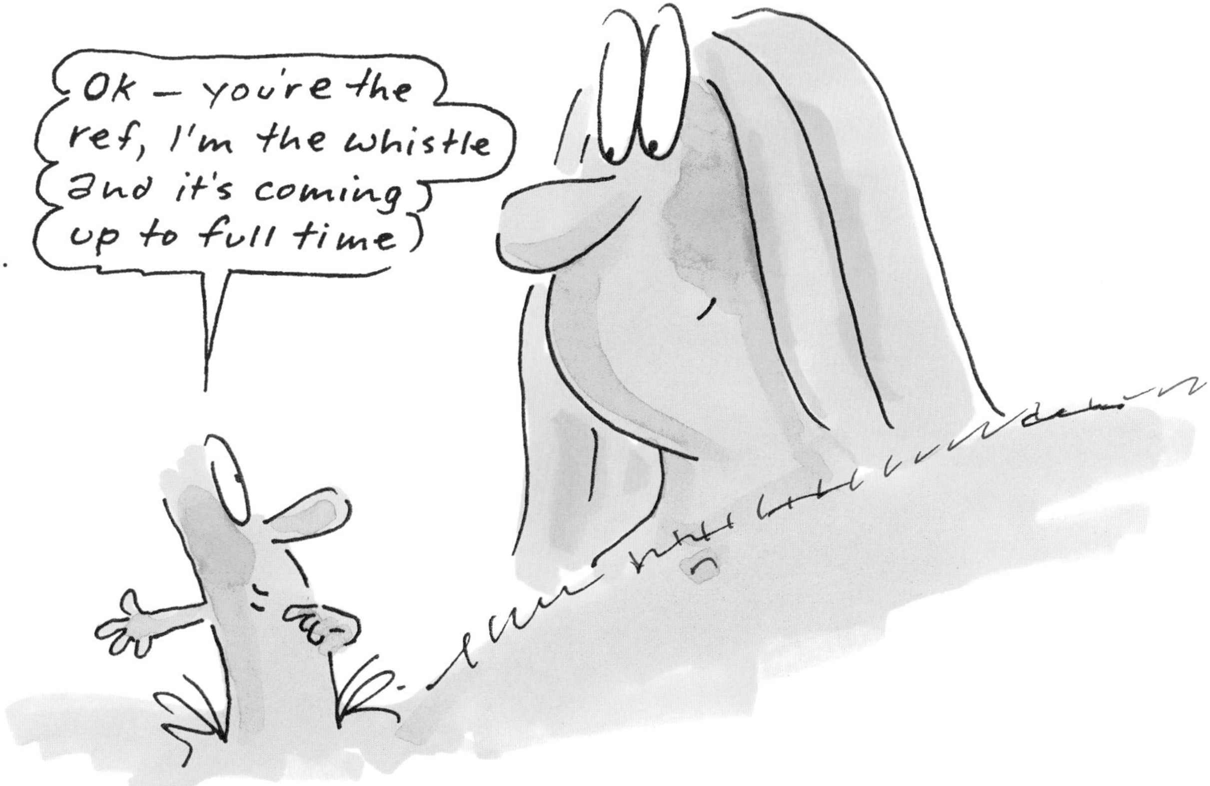
Ok – you're the ref, I'm the whistle and it's coming up to full time

Seduction

Whatever you wear under your jeans is a bit hit or miss. You may be lucky and be wearing y-fronts on the very day you get intimate with a girl who has a passion for men in y-fronts.

More likely, however, the girl you're with won't like your choice of underpants be they boxers or thong, so be prepared by putting on several pairs of different types. Very cool.

Your t-shirt can say a lot about you, particularly if it has a message on the front so you can say it all without having to open your mouth. A t-shirt that proclaims HARD DICK, EASY LAY will give her a clear idea that you're a direct, uncomplicated sort of chap. Go through a checklist before you leave home: Have you got her favourite wine, your toothbrush, money, good looks, talent? If you are short on any of these, get some immediately.

I said offer to buy her a drink – not offer her money!

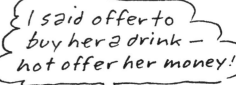

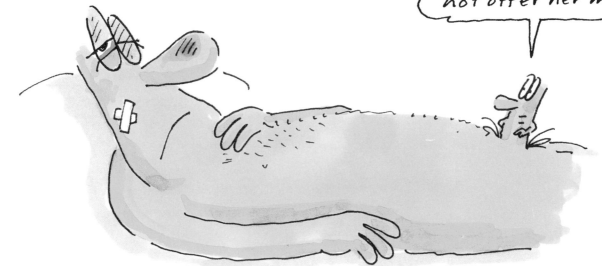

Girls - stare at this spiral for two minutes...

You are now in a state of deep hypnosis. Take off your clothes and lie down. You will wake up when you hear snoring

Actually doing it

This is the dirty bit. Or should be if you're doing it right, as the aptly named Woody would say.

As a man and woman gradually get to know each other it will dawn on them that there are ways to do it other than 'doggy' style. For example, if you can bear the sight of each other you can experiment and try it face to face, with her on her back and him face down on top. This is called the 'missionary' position and if they would only admit to it, a lot of couples do it this way all the time. It is actually quite nice once you get over the initial shock.

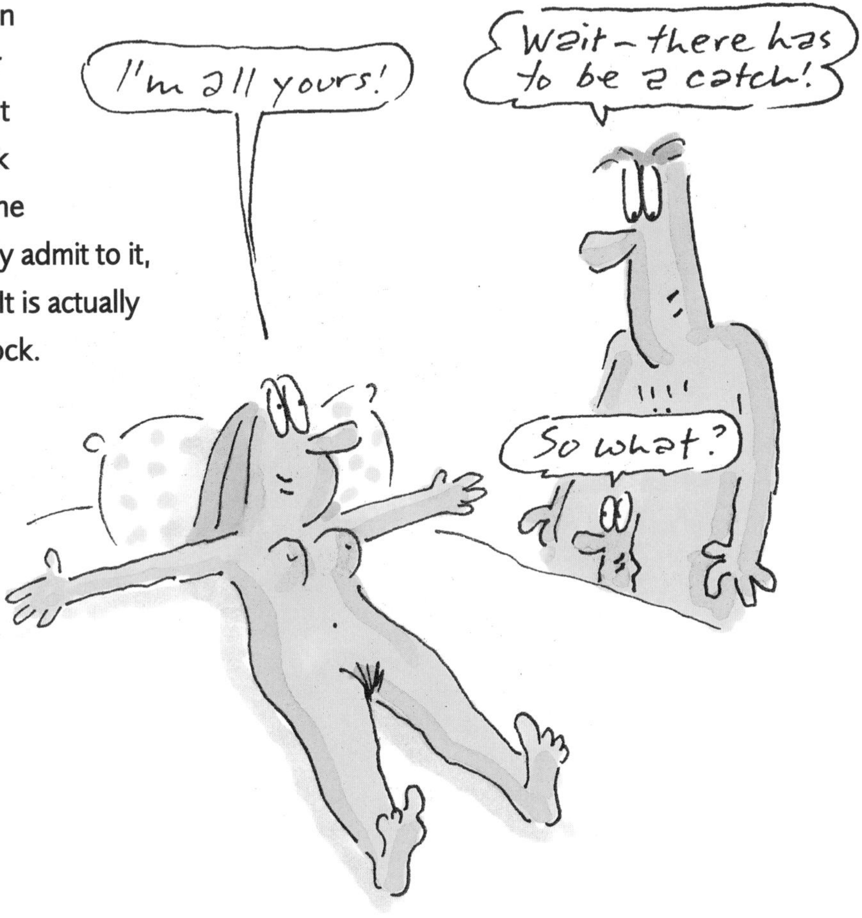
I'm all yours!
Wait – there has to be a catch!
So what?

Actually Willie has a lot of other, more exotic, ideas that many people tend to overlook in their haste to get it over with. Willie puts it down to laziness, and if he had things all his own way there would be no limit to the variety of shocking tableaux in the boudoir.

For one thing, Willie likes early nights and in his opinion there are many more interesting things to do with the midnight oil than burn it.

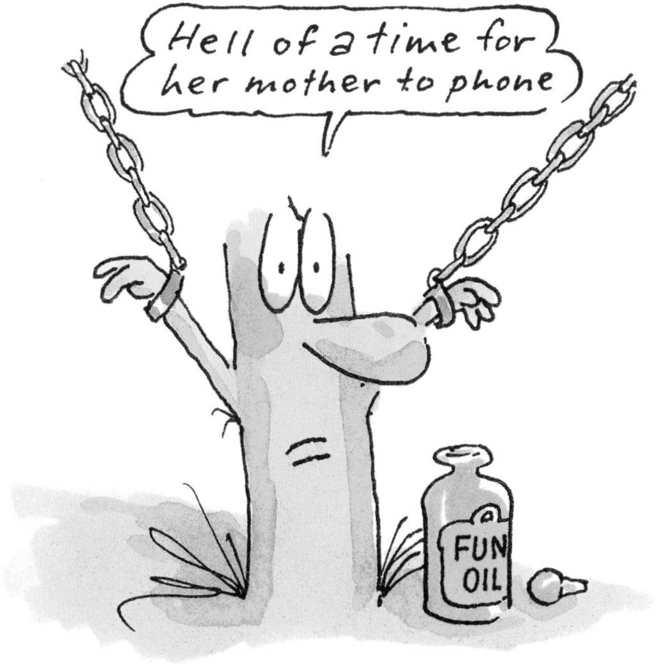
Hell of a time for her mother to phone
FUN OIL

Oral sex

Oral sex is a unique thrill, and even if you're not feeling hungry you will soon work up an appetite.

If you ever find yourself with a strange set of symptoms such as sore tongue, lockjaw, neck ache, impaired vision, loss of hearing or crushed skull and wonder why, you are probably indulging in oral sex.

Nice as it is, you can overdo it, so do warming-up exercises first. Try bending forward at 90 degrees, placing your face on the wall. Stick your tongue out and wiggle it till you scream.

How does it feel to be a phallic symbol that only gets eaten once?

Oral sex doesn't do you any favours in morning's early light – your face looks like a glazed doughnut

Strange stuff

Willie insists that we put this in, and you know what he's like. It's what keeps the sex shops and the drug stores in business.

Some people like getting dressed up, tied up, hung up and God knows what else. Anything to make a change from the routine of missionaries and dogs. It's up to the individual what fantasy turns them on most, but talking about it can be embarrassing. One feels such a fool persuading a loved one to dress up as a rabbit and getting arrested for indulging in an indecent display in McDonalds. Or you could find yourself in bed with one of your lovers, their attractive friend, a jar of honey and a wooden spatula. Wait a minute – Willie says that sounds like a good one.

Most interesting drugs are illegal, but you can do anything you like with aspirin, antacids, styling mousse and vitamin tablets. Wow.

Sex toys are widely used these days, and at some length too. Don't forget the batteries run out after only six hours of continuous use.

Something you always wanted to know but were afraid to ask..

EROTICA

PORN

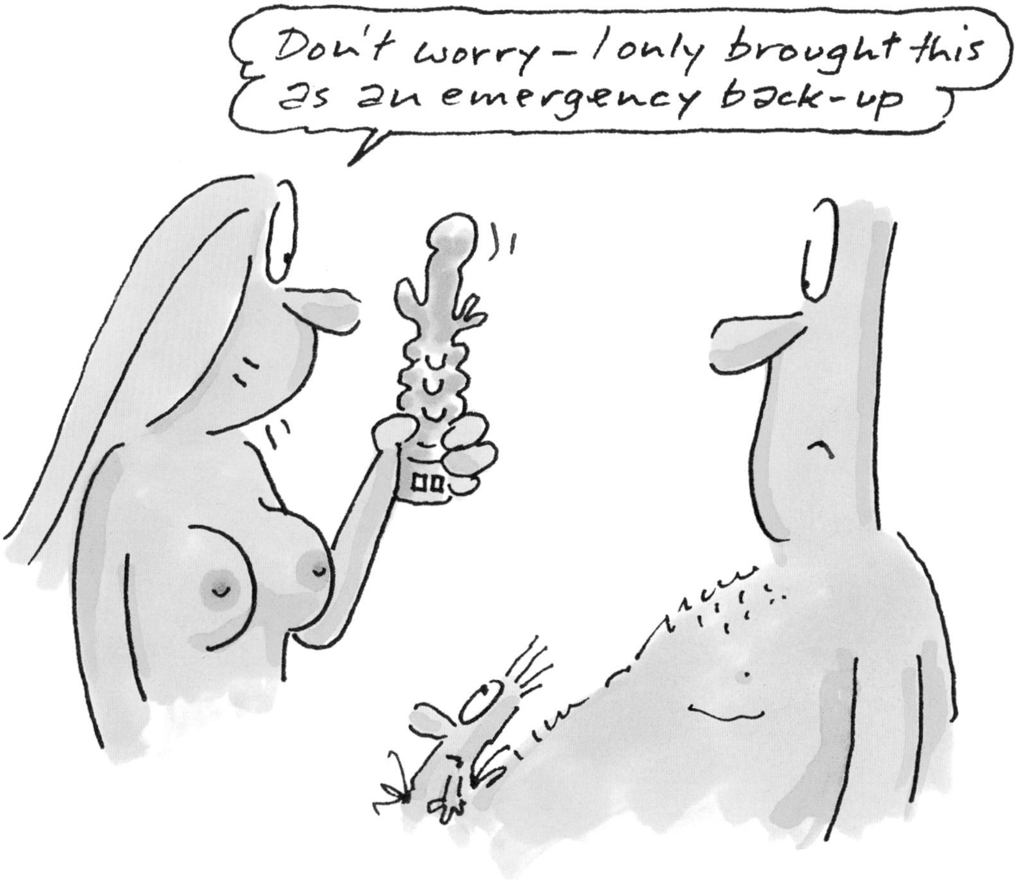
Don't worry – I only brought this as an emergency back-up

Safe sex

Wicked Willie's idea of safe sex is when her husband is away on business. But there are many other methods.

The safest form of sex is the 'withdrawal' method: the moment she gets that suggestive glint in her eye, he withdraws to a safe distance.

Safe but unlikely Willie says.

Condoms come in all kinds of flavours these days. Favourites are lemon, strawberry, plain rubber and cheese and onion. Cheese and ham never caught on since it tastes exactly like Willie.

As you may have guessed, Willie loathes condoms and the unnatural barrier that comes between him and his natural environment. It infuriates him in the extreme if anyone dresses him up in one, and he gets his own back by curling up and going to sleep. Revenge is sweet F.A.

The pill is ok except for the fact that it keeps falling out. Then there's other stuff too boring to talk about. What's next?

Sorry, but I don't do rubber

I cant make up my mind between the pink and the blue – what do you think?
I don't care – you choose
How about green? She's into ecology
... or possibly black – it's very dramatic
RING RING
Hello Judy? What??.. you can't?
All dressed up and nowhere to go

Can't get it up

It happens to every man at one time or another. How often have you heard that tired old cliché? You know that feeling when the girl of your dreams finally gives in and there she is naked in bed next to you and the cut-out in your brain overloads and Willie gets his jammies on and goes bye-byes?

You DO?

You're drunk.

You haven't been drinking?

My God! See a specialist immediately.

And while we're on the subject of drink...

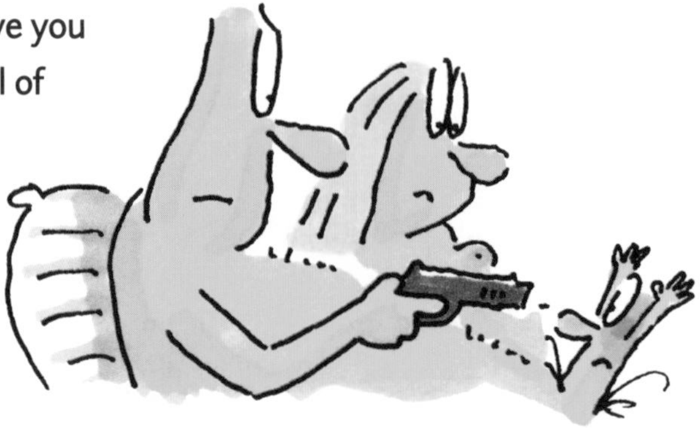

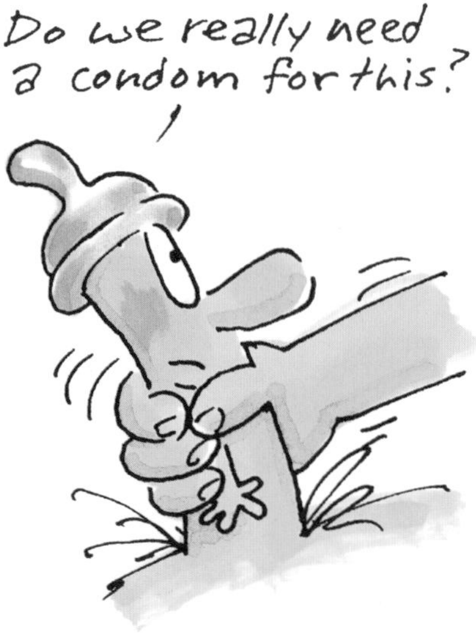
Do we really need a condom for this?

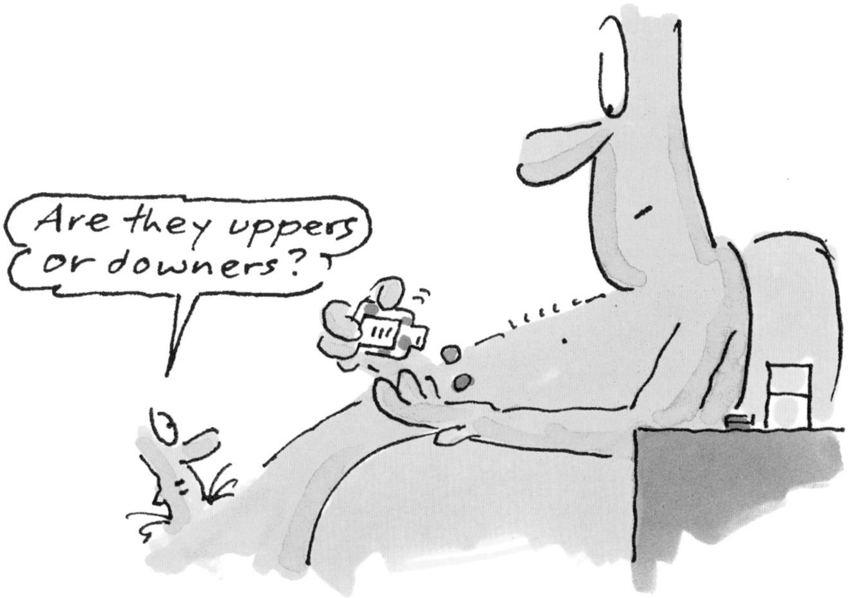
Are they uppers or downers?

Alcohol

Although a certain amount of drink can be the stairway to heaven, overdo it and it can also be Man's Best Friend's worst enemy. Sure, a relaxing bottle or two is ok and it will liberate your mouth and oil the parts that say amusing things. Chat-up gets more fluent with the flow of booze, and it will also do amazing things to the female libido.

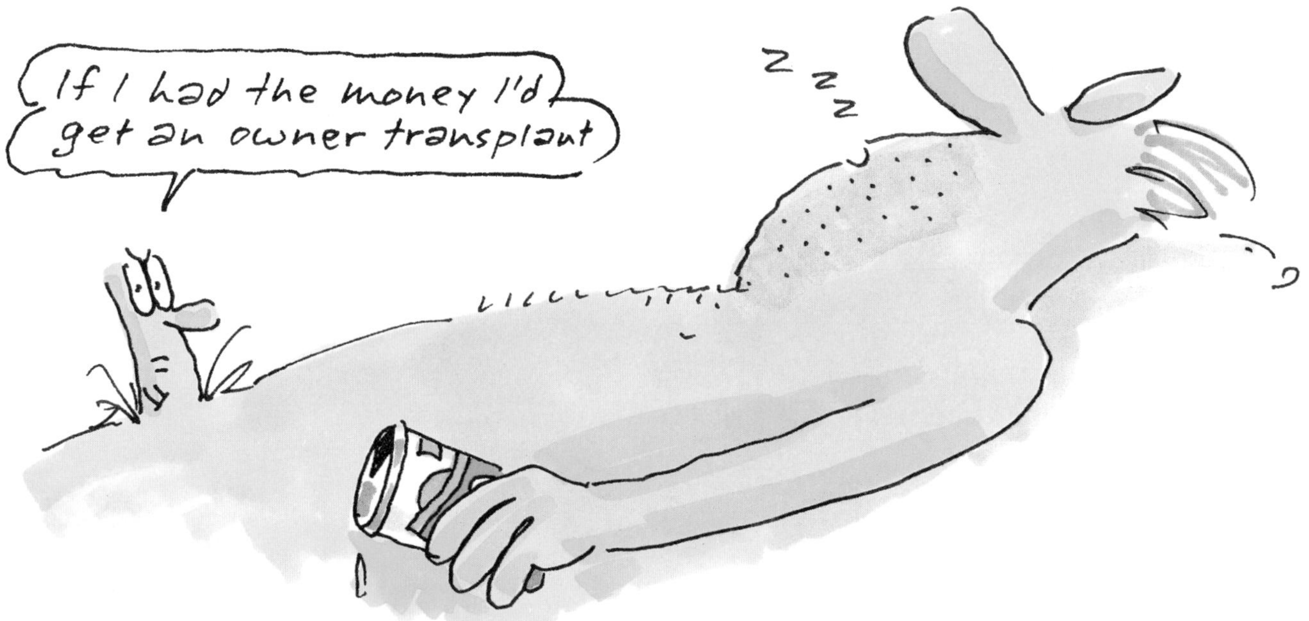
If I had the money I'd get an owner transplant
Z Z Z

Knowing when to stop is the trick. Too much and Willie may refuse to come out and play. Or his slave will behave in some disgraceful fashion and his intended victim will call a cab. Either way, in the morning she won't be there, but Willie will – ready for anything as usual. His man will be suffering from yet another hangover and hating himself for blowing it again.

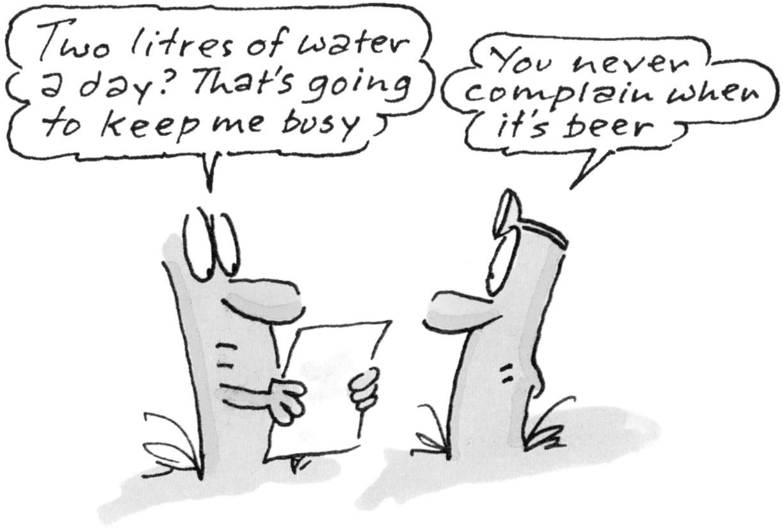
Two litres of water a day? That's going to keep me busy
You never complain when it's beer

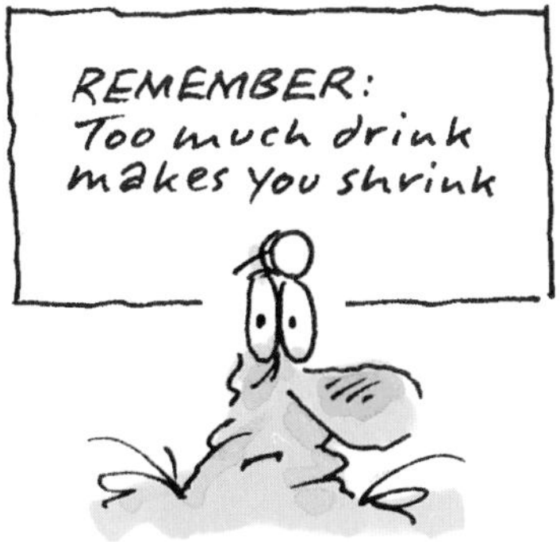
REMEMBER: Too much drink makes you shrink

So stay below the medically recommended 201 units, spaced sensibly throughout the day. If you are on the road, remember the dangers and try and drag yourself to the footpath. If you are driving, do yourself a huge favour and keep a sharp eye out for the police. Many an accident has been caused by holding a bottle in the left hand and trying to steer with the right while the other is on your girlfriend's knee.

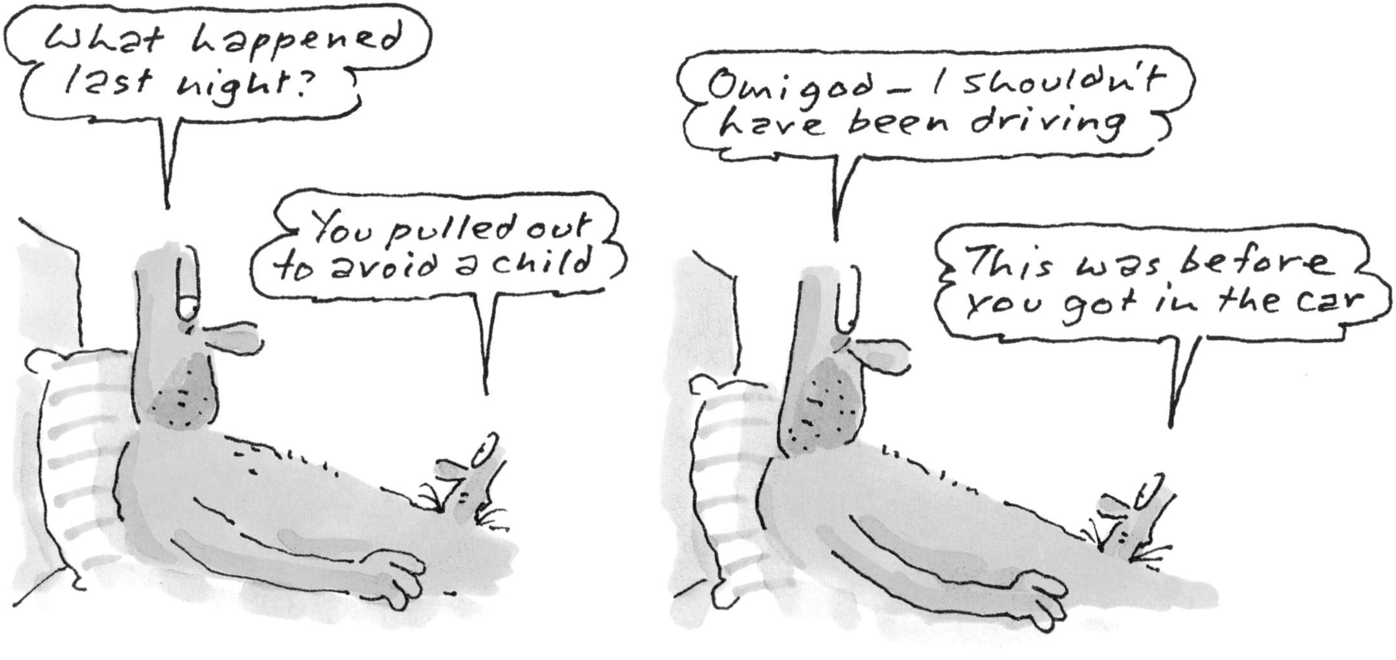
What happened last night?
You pulled out to avoid a child
Omigod – I shouldn't have been driving
This was before you got in the car

So what happens to you sperm after a vasectomy operation?
Oh we just hang out on our redundancy money - in bars mainly
we talk about football
And we watch girls - Guy stuff
It's the romance and tenderness, I miss
Theres always one

You drink too much
It smooths out wrinkles and tones the body
No it doesn't
Yes it does
In fact, one more whisky and you'll be Britney Spears

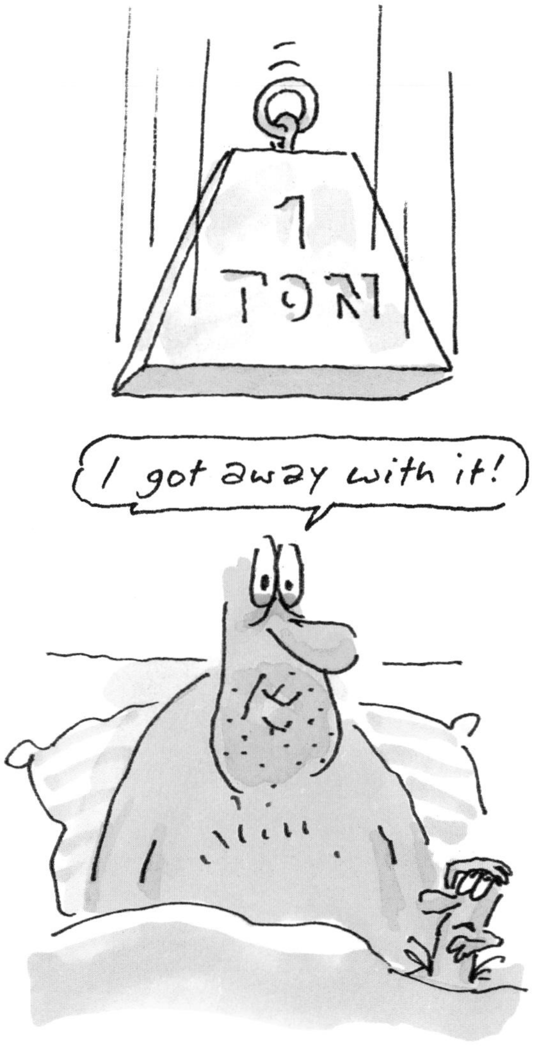
1 TON
I got away with it!

The joy of DIY

DIY sex is what happens when nothing else happens, i.e. most of the time. Willie would be lost without it, since normally the only person he ever gets lucky with is his clunky alter ego.

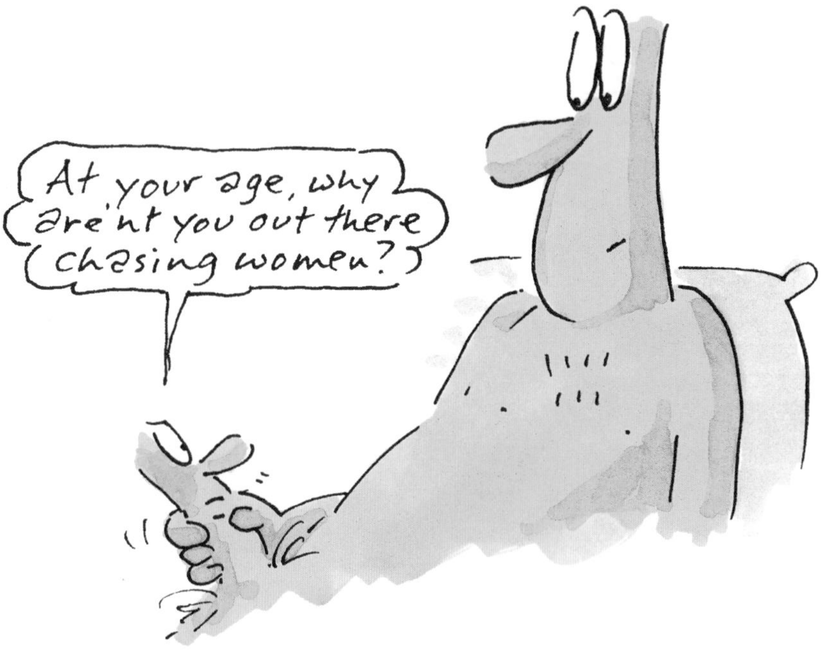
At your age, why are'nt you out there chasing women?

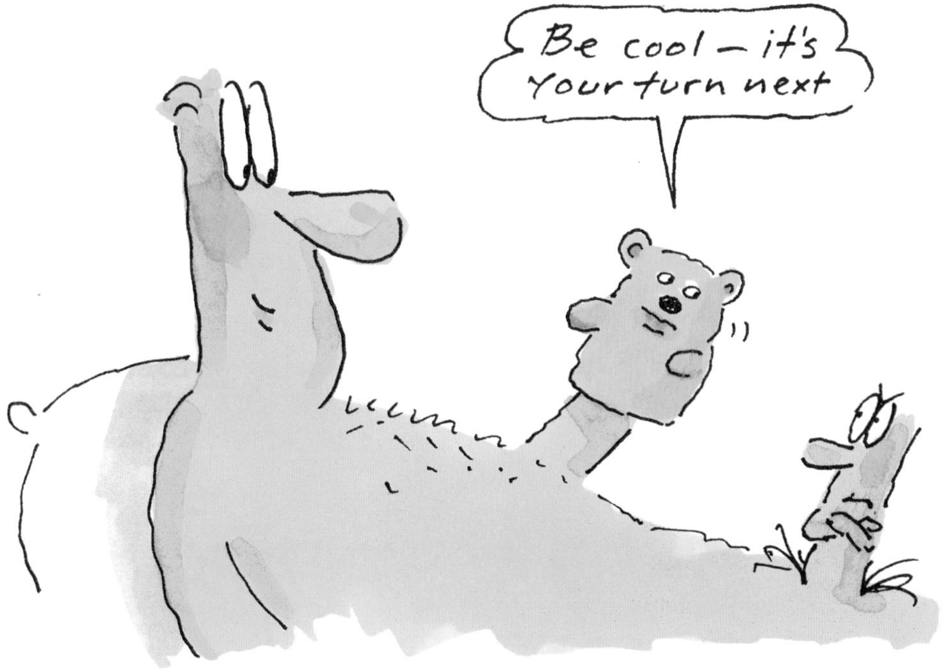
Be cool – it's Your turn next

You know what we're talking about here – yes, the solitary vice. Historically, it was discovered by Onan, a biblical character who 'spilled his seed on the ground'. That's why Dorothy Parker named her budgie after him. According to the historian M. Brooks, Onan stumbled one day while strolling in the desert and, to stop himself falling, grabbed the first thing that came to hand. Thus Onan and Willie became firm friends and started a trend. M***********n is perfectly normal and not a filthy dirty habit. An estimated 100 per cent of people do it, which is way above average and goes to show what a filthy dirty bunch we are.

Here's a secret: girls do it as much as boys and sometimes more.
But who can blame them.

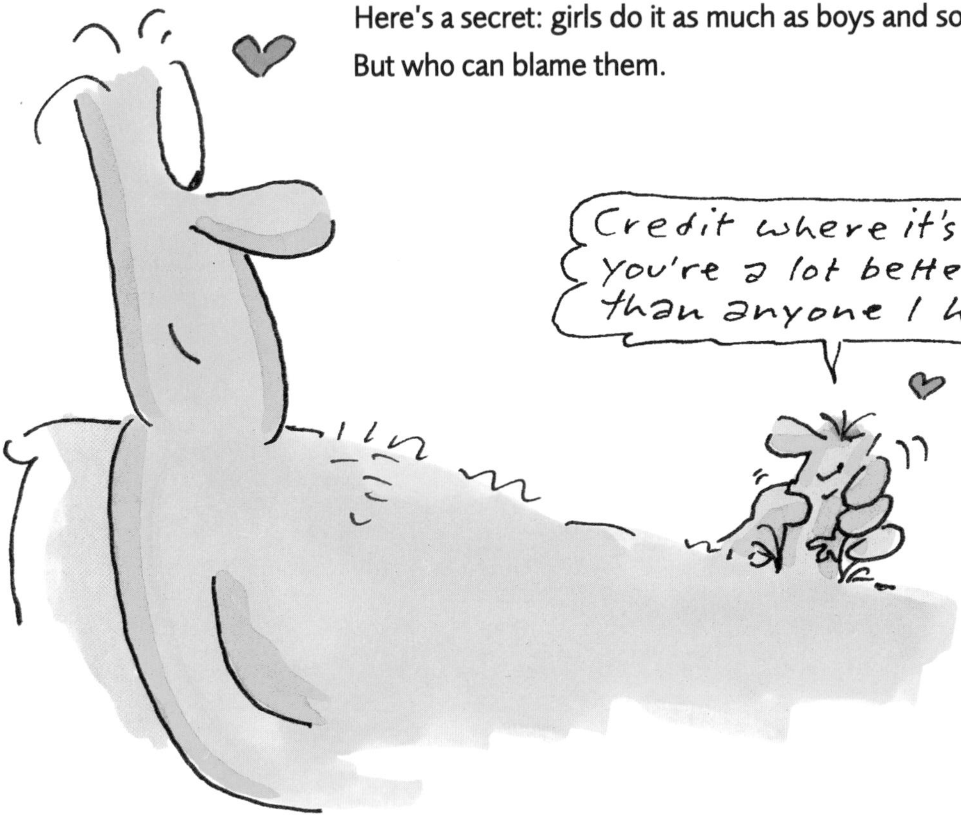
Credit where it's due, chief – you're a lot better at this than anyone I know

Most women don't mind if their man plays with Willie as it saves them time and trouble. But others hate it because they can hardly complain about being a sex object if he's continually treating himself as one.

Other advantages of DIY are:

* You can have anyone you want.
* You don't have to take your hand shopping first.
* Your hand never says 'no'.

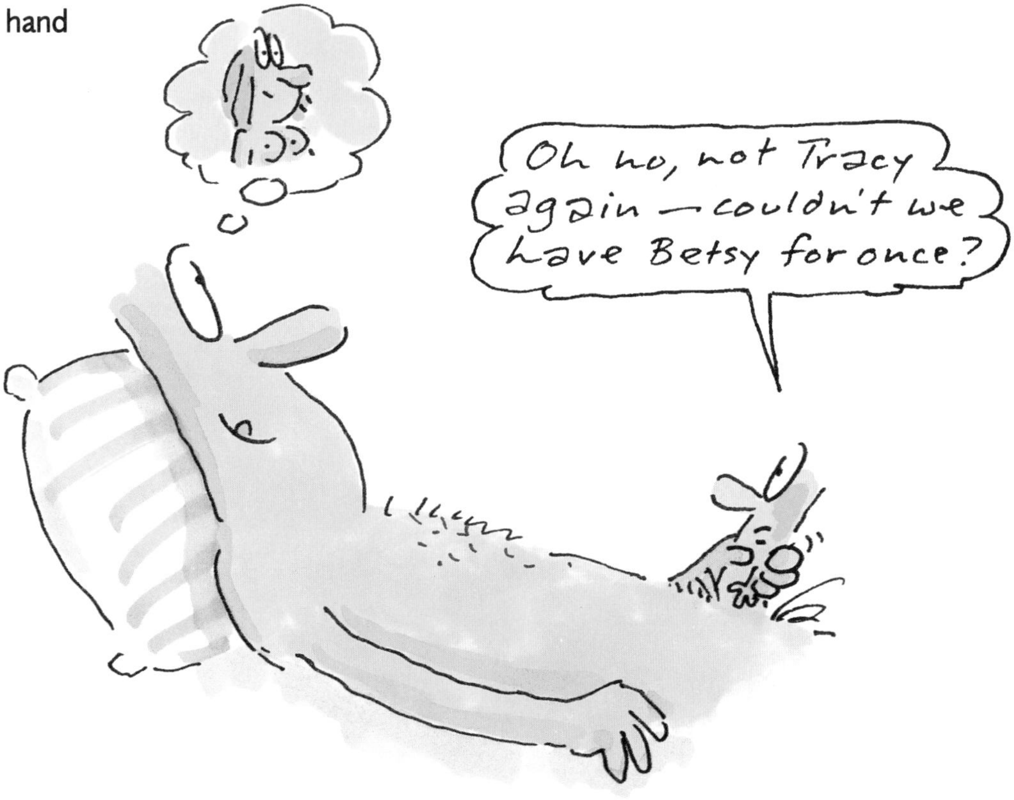
Oh no, not Tracy again – couldn't we have Betsy for once?

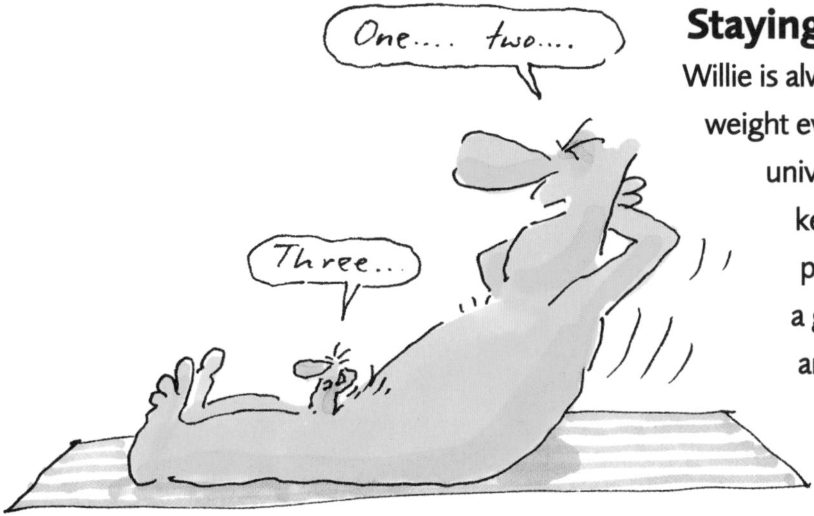
One.... two....
Three...

Staying healthy

Willie is always young and healthy and never puts on weight even when his slave is expanding faster than the universe. However it is in Willie's best interests to keep the idiot in reasonable shape if only for pulling purposes. Regular check-ups are ok as it's a good opportunity to meet nice young nurses, and dieting is neither here nor there to Willie. But exercise is another matter, as Willie has no choice other than to go along for the ride.

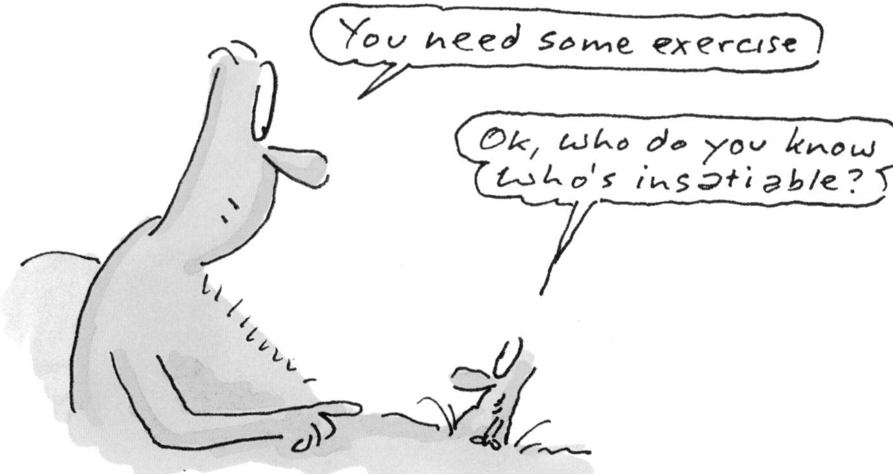
You need some exercise
Ok, who do you know who's insatiable?

As the odd couple get older, the big one starts to lose the use of his brain. He gets just as many ideas, but sadly they're not all that bright. It seems that a man's maturity and wisdom are no contest against the will of the enemy below who never wants to give up and call it a day.

Beware of boredom. If a man has nothing particular to do, and is just hanging out, perhaps on holiday, his mind pleasantly off-guard, he is vulnerable to a senior Willie moment. Just the thought of sex, the merest glimpse of a nubile female shape... and he's got you by the goolies!

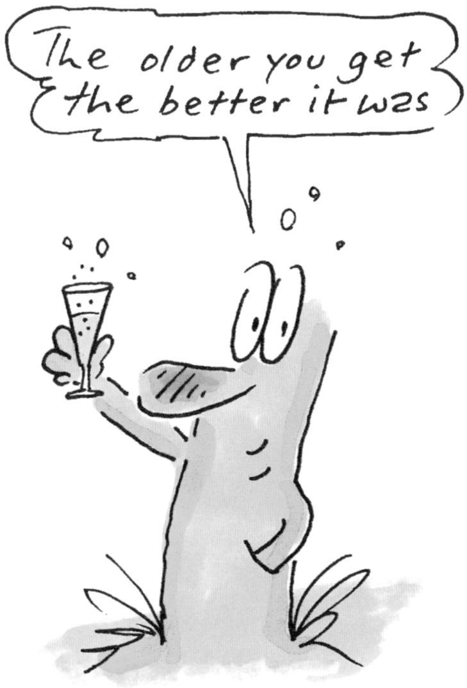
The older you get the better it was

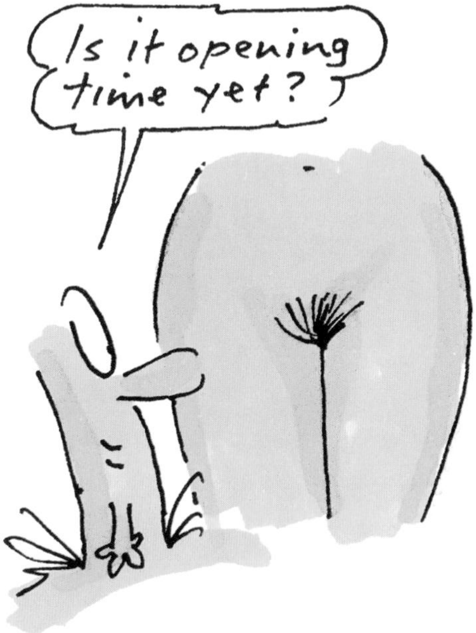
Is it opening time yet?